Praise for *The Lay of Old Hex*

The spectral balladry of Adam Bolivar is a refreshing adaptation of the ballads of Sir Walter Scott, Thomas Moore, and other Romantic poets who found in them an ideal vehicle for the powerful expression of weird moods and imagery. Bolivar's flawless metre and smooth-flowing stanzas create a sense of cumulative terror and strangeness easily rivaling the best work of contemporary weird fiction writers.—S. T. Joshi

Adam Bolivar emanates invocatory chants that summon us to dark worlds just the other side of the existential page. Go with him. If you don't come back alive, you'll at least be somewhere quite interesting indeed.—John Shirley, author of *Lovecraft Alive!*

Adam Bolivar's ballads are doorways to worlds of light and darkness steeped in tradition and folklore and yet infused with a freshness and life all their own. To read his work is to journey to realms where the sunlight ever lies in pools of honey, Old Scratch lurks in every shadow, and dreams and nightmares walk the ways of Ye Yellow'd Reed.—D. L. Myers

Adam Bolivar's work represents a deft fusion of echoes from folk tale and nursery rhyme with old legendry and hoary mystery. In his use of balladry, a form to which we are largely unaccustomed in this day and age, he has single-handedly forged a resurgence of the form. *The Lay of Old Hex*, with its mixture and interweaving of poetry and prose, and its interconnected episodes, will intrigue and delight all who appreciate the weird and wonderful in poesy.—Leigh Blackmore, author of *Spores from Sharnoth and Other Madnesses*

Adam Bolivar offers a unique blend of folktale, fantasy, and pure cosmic horror in this well-crafted collection. Musical yet accessible, the traditional ballad is ideal for story-telling. As Jack's generations roll by, readers will find themselves taken with—and by—these tricksters of the silver key. High entertainment for any fan of the fantastic!—Ann K. Schwader

A thoroughly different look at the Appalachian take on English folktales, *The Lay of Old Hex* meanders through fantasy literature from nursery rhymes to Stephen King. Always interesting and intelligent, and occasionally brilliantly effective.—David Drake, author of *Old Nathan*

The Lay of Old Hex, is a stunning achievement. Adam Bolivar writes what at first glance appear to be traditional supernatural ballads adhering to an archaic formalism. But they are in fact fully modern, 21st century works, moving far beyond the constraints of the last century's almost universal free verse ethic to create wondrous visions of Gothic weirdness using every tool available to a contemporary poet, including rhyme, meter, alliteration, metaphor, allegory, musicality, mythology, and the rich and quirky historical traditions of Appalachian and Scottish balladry. Bolivar seems to have been born to resurrect the ballad as a vital force in weird literature. He comes to this task as a fully developed practitioner of his unique art. The poems are flawlessly executed, remarkably engaging, and endlessly delightful. He will be imitated, but not equaled.
—David Barker, author (with W. H. Pugmire) of *The Revenant of Rebecca Pascal* and *In the Gulfs of Dream and Other Lovecraftian Tales*.

To read the work of Adam Bolivar is to enter an enchanted realm of pure poetry, where skill is combined with a brilliant imagination. Superb!
—W. H. Pugmire

Come, take a journey with Jack as you read these extraordinary heroic ballads Bolivar has written with finesse. These tales will take you through haunting adventures involving eldritch mariners and Old Scratch. Come, take a seat in this rocking chair and let the Black Shepherd guide you through these macabre tales.—Ashley Dioses, author of *Diary of a Sorceress*

The Lay of Old Hex

Hippocampus Press Library of Poetry

R. H. Barlow, *Eyes of the God: The Weird Fiction and Poetry*, ed. S. T. Joshi, Douglas A. Anderson, and David E. Schultz

Park Barnitz, *The Book of Jade: A New Critical Edition*, compiled by David E. Schultz and Michael J. Abolafia

Ashley Dioses, *Diary of a Sorceress*

Michael Fantina, *Alchemy of Dreams and Other Poems*

Nora May French, *The Outer Gate: The Collected Poems*, ed. Donald Sidney-Fryer and Alan Gullette

Wade German, *Dreams from a Black Nebula*

Alan Gullette, *Intimations of Unreality: Weird Fiction and Poetry*

R. Nemo Hill, *The Strange Music of Erich Zann*

S. T. Joshi and Steven J. Mariconda, ed. *Dreams of Fear: Poetry of Terror and the Supernatural*

H. P. Lovecraft, *The Ancient Track: The Complete Poetical Works*, ed. S. T. Joshi

Samuel Loveman, *Out of the Immortal Night: Selected Works*, ed. S. T. Joshi and David E. Schultz

H. L. Mencken, *Collected Poems*, ed. S. T. Joshi

K. A. Opperman, *The Crimson Tome*

Fred Phillips, *From the Cauldron*

———, *Winds from Sheol*

Anne K. Schwader, *Twisted in Dream: The Collected Weird Poetry*

Clark Ashton Smith, *The Hashish-Eater*, ed. with notes, &c., by Donald Sidney-Fryer

———, *The Last Oblivion: Best Fantastic Poems*, ed. S. T. Joshi and David E. Schultz

———, *The Complete Poetry and Translations*, ed. S. T. Joshi and David E. Schultz

George Sterling, *Complete Poetry*, ed. S. T. Joshi and David E. Schultz

———, *The Thirst of Satan: Poems of Fantasy and Terror*, ed. S. T. Joshi

Donald Sidney-Fryer, *The Atlantis Fragments: The Trilogy of Songs and Sonnets Atlantean*

———, *Odds and Ends*

———, *Ends and Odds*

Donald Wandrei, *Sanctity and Sin: The Collected Poems and Prose Poems*, ed. S. T. Joshi

S. T. Joshi, ed., *Spectral Realms* (2014–)

Adam Bolivar

The Lay of Old Hex

Spectral Ballads & Weird Jack Tales

Hippocampus Press
New York

The Lay of Old Hex: Spectral Ballads & Weird Jack Tales
© 2017 by Hippocampus Press
Works by Adam Bolivar © 2017 by Adam Bolivar
Introduction © 2017 by K. A. Opperman

All Rights Reserved. No part of this work may be reproduced in any form or by any means without the written permission of the publisher.

Published by Hippocampus Press
P.O. Box 641, New York, NY 10156
http://www.hippocampuspress.com

Cover design and restoration of vintage interior illustrations by Dan Sauer, dansauerdesign.com
Hippocampus Press logo designed by Anastasia Damianakos.

First Edition
1 3 5 7 9 8 6 4 2

ISBN 978-1-61498-198-5

Contents

Preface 13

Introduction: The Lay of Adam Bolivar, *by* K. A. Opperman 15

    I. The Ballad of Jack Keeper 19

    II. The Black Cup 21

    III. The Lay of Jackson Drake 37

    IV. The Dream Emerald 53

    V. The Broken Promise 83

    VI. Gooseberry Tea 97

    VII. Jack the Hunter 107

    VIII. Fiddler Jack 113

    IX. Jack, a Key, and Dreame 123

    X. Jack in Y^e Dreame 127

    XI. Death Came to Hexham 139

    XII. Y^e Yellow'd Reed 147

    XIII. Jack and the Devil 151

    XIV. The Lay of Old Hex 163

    XV. The Ineffable Journey of Jasper Drake 169

    XVI. Jack in the Witch House 185

    XVII. Jack and the Giants 199

    XVIII. The Hexham Horror 207

    XIX. The Ballad of Harold Gloom 221

    XX. The Devil's Lanthorn 227

XXI. The Ballad of Jack Drake	231
XXII. The Grimalkin's Curse	245
XXIII. The Black Tree	253
XXIV. The Death of Arthur Drake	265
XXV. Scarlett Cloake	271
XXVI. The Pixy-Wife	277
XXVII. The Lay of King Marock	283
XXVIII. The Unquiet Grave	291
XXIX. Black Star	299
XXX. The Dream-Quest of Unknown Jack	303
XXXI. The Rime of the Eldritch Mariner	307
XXXII. An Ancient Tomb A-Yonder Lies	313
XXXIII. Y^e Jack of War	319
Acknowledgments	327

*To Jasper, my only son,
I leave a silver key . . .*

Child Roland to the dark tower came,
His word was still—Fie, foh and fum,
I smell the blood of a British man.
 —*King Lear*, Act 3, Scene 4

PREFACE

In 1777, driven from his native Virginia by revolutionary upheaval, David "The Tory" Hicks settled on the banks of the Watauga River, deep in the Appalachian wilderness of western North Carolina. Hicks carried with him a venerable English tradition of fireside tales about Jack, a trickster-hero who fells giants, bests witches and outwits the Devil himself—tales that were enjoying a resurgence in that century on the pages of cheaply printed chapbooks illustrated with woodcut engravings—the forerunners of modern comic books.

But it was Council Harmon (1806-1890), David Hicks' great-grandson, who crystallized the oral tradition of the "Jack tales" collected by folklorist Richard Chase from families in that region in the 1930s. These tales had been handed down from generation to generation like precious heirlooms, retold in the colorful dialect of the Scotch-Irish immigrants who had migrated to the Appalachians in the late 1700s and early 1800s. Council Harmon's masterstroke was to take the original English stories and combine them with the Märchen brought over by the German settlers, whose blood also ran in his veins. Isolated from the world at large, the mountain-hemmed valley where the Watauga River flowed had become a walled garden of storytelling. Added to the mix of English and German influences was a rich tradition of balladry bequeathed by the so-called "Scotch-Irish" who came from the borderlands of England and Scotland: ballads of misty northern legends of elf queens, dæmon lovers and spectral curses. It was fertile ground for Jack's beanstalk to grow and sprout new shoots.

And so, I begin the cycle anew. Reforging this rich legacy on my own poetic anvil, I have found the folklore surprisingly malleable, able to take on fantastic new shapes while retaining its essential integrity. I can weave strands of Jack tales into any number of folk narratives—Childe Roland, Arthurian legends, even the cosmic horror of H. P. Lovecraft. In keeping with tradition, I write my ballads in quatrains of alternating lines of iambic tetrameter (eight syllables) and iambic trimeter (six syllables), rhymed either ABCB or ABAB. As Sir Walter Scott, Samuel Taylor Coleridge and other Romantic poets before me found, ballad meter gives me access to haunted undercurrents of folk memory, allowing me to produce spectral effects rarely found in other forms of weird literature.

When reading these verses aloud (which I strongly encourage the reader to do), please note the word "Y^e" is pronounced the same as the modern "the"—not "yee" as is often mistakenly believed. A "lay," for the curious, is another word for a ballad or narrative poem. May Jack's journey continue for many centuries to come, in whatever form he (or she) may take . . .

—ADAM BOLIVAR

Portland, Oregon
28 July 2017

INTRODUCTION: THE LAY OF ADAM BOLIVAR

I first became aware of the name Adam Bolivar through that most noteworthy journal of weird and supernatural poetry, *Spectral Realms*. His entry in the first issue, "The Hidden God," immediately stood out to me, not only because of its exceptional length but also because of its fantastical fairytale imagery and its formal rhyming structure. Here was a kindred soul, I thought; a poet not far removed from my own sensibilities.

In time—and not much, at that—we began to correspond regularly via the usual modern avenues of email and social media. After all, we were both writers for the same journal, and seemed to share similar Lovecraftian leanings and poetic tendencies. He naturally began to fall into place among the tight-knit poets' circle of which I was a part, and soon became its fourth and final primary member. I refer to the Crimson Circle...a name coined by Mr. Bolivar himself; and at the last H. P. Lovecraft Film Festival to be held in San Pedro, California—approaching the midnight hour on Walpurgis Eve—the Circle was sealed. With the tracing, anointing, and subsequent burning of the sigil we named the Crimson Sign—with the chanting of an auspicious poem, and an appeal to the Black Shepherd himself—our Pact was forged.

Among contemporary scribes of fantastical poetry—of which there are perhaps now more than ever before—none stand out in quite the same darkly whimsical way as Adam Bolivar. A marionettist who has proclaimed Weird balladry his especial province, he is equally adept at pulling the strings of language to produce a chimerical effect, as he is at weaving into his verses the strands of an obscure, yet hauntingly familiar folklore. His is a folklore fraught with black magic, the restless ghost of childhood dreams, and a tainted whimsy wherein the Devil is an old friend. In these poems, the primal stuff of our Collective Unconscious bubbles up from the very Cauldron of Sorcery, reawakening the old, old dreams that Mr. Bolivar, in the present volume, helps us to remember.

Perhaps the most immediately striking aspect of this remarkable collection is the interweaving ballads and prose tales. This form is rarely employed, yet it seems especially suited to Bolivar's particular brand of storytelling. As with any mixed-media work of art, each element informs the other; the poems lending musical interludes that add a sort of backdrop or undercurrent to the stories, and the stories providing a mythical landscape in which these poems can truly thrive and most fully work their magic. In this way the pace is nicely varied, though the tone remains consistent—one of black enchantment, and dim, haunted wonder.

The narratives herein, whether they be prose or poetry, largely concern the doings of Jack, the giant-killing Everyman from time immemorial, and related members of the decadent House of Drake. These folk-currents are skillfully interwoven with Lovecraftian elements, producing an amalgam as unique as it is *haunting*. I do not use the latter adjective lightly; these tales take the reader to dim locales beyond the borders of dream, and linger long after the book has been shut. Familiar fairytale tropes and figures, too, lend their timeless impact to the mixture in an unprecedented feat of literary alchemy. What's more, these seemingly disparate elements do not clash; rather, they are all made to seem completely *natural* beside and amid one another. No matter how outlandish the narrative becomes—and it does—all feels perfectly in place. And this, I must point out, is the mark of a skilled storyteller.

In this age of looser and increasingly experimental poetic expressions, it is ever more vital that a select few step up to bear the torch of Tradition. Adam Bolivar, using the ballad—a most simple yet powerful form that has proven its mettle over several centuries—is clearly one of these stewards of the old ways. Bringing a traditional narrative mode into a new light, and reinvigorating it with a fresh subject matter—yet one that rings true and pure, and organically evolved from the folk balladry of yore—Bolivar competently bears the torch, and marches it forward into a new century, as one of the key Dark Romantics who are spearheading the ineluctable resurgence of formal poetry. As such, I think it is safe to say that the Lay of Adam Bolivar shall be sung for many generations to come.

—K. A. OPPERMAN

Anaheim, California
13 August 2017

Jack Keeper

– I –
The Ballad of Jack Keeper

This is the ballad of stingy Jack Keeper,
Always a step ahead of the Reaper.
The further he swam, he sank a bit deeper;
Hear ye the wages of poor old Jack Keeper:

He hoarded his gold in a tattered silk bag,
His shoes shot with holes, his shirt a torn rag.
The floors of his house had carpets of dust,
He served his few guests a handful of crust.

Jack watered his wine, he skimped on his tea;
Not sugar or milk could anyone see.
Pinching all of his pennies to slag,
He had for a wife a doddering hag.

To save himself ink, Jack wrote with his blood;
To spill a small cup to Jack was a flood.
Drinking of course, he did very little;
His skin was quite dry, his bones very brittle.

No children at all did run through Jack's house,
So cold was inside, it kept not a mouse.
No embers of wood on the fireplace burned,
And under the covers the missus was spurned.

No horses were groomed inside of Jack's stable,
The dogs were long dead from begging at table.
The cats had all fled to chase other mice;
The only thing living perhaps were some lice.

Bare bones for a body, a skull for a head,
The plague struck at last; Jack Keeper was dead.
Nobody wept or dug him a grave,
No death knell was rung for his soul to be saved.
To wander the earth shall be Jack's black fate,
Looking for food his hunger to sate.

– II –
THE BLACK CUP

Oneset upawn a time, not such a very lawng time ago, I lived in a church-house with my Ma Daisy, an I was her only chile. We was a-livin in a church-house on account of my grampa he was a preecher. But he was lawng since gone up in to hevvin an the church was now jest a house, though it still had bells in the steeple, of the kind that go jingle-jangle on Sundays, though I can't recollect the last time that they did.

I can't recollect my Pa neither, on account of he expired for I was even popped out of my Ma, when I was jest a bun in her oven so as to speak. Mum's the word with my Ma, allus is. All I was ever able to squeeze out of her was that he was some kind of up on a high hoss gennleman, an that he'd a-come all the way over from Merry Old England. An I also know that his name was Drake, on account of that's my name too. Jack Drake, at your services.

I was sompin of a no-account layabout, an I shood a helped my Ma more with the chores an suchlike, her bein a widder an all. But I was all ways a-climbin trees when I shood a bin choppin wood, an a-snoozin in the sun when I shood a bin carryin water. But Ma was a forgivin soal. A real angel. She done give me milk an cake when she shood a bin whuppin my backside, an told me pixy tales when she shood a bin tannin my hide.

Then one day she gives me a basket full of apples, an tells me to take em on down to Hexum Town an see if I can't fetch a few coppers fer em. We was awful pur, an a few coppers was like a king's ransum to us. So I put on my battered old hat, an head on down the road to Hexum.

It is such a bee-you-tea-full mornin an the sun beat down so hot it is all I can do not to eat them red juicy apples in that basket of mine. But I

21

didn't want to let my Ma down, so I keep on keepin on a-luggin that old thing down the dry an dusty road. Round about halfway down the road I comes to a fork in the road. A cloof in the hoof so as to speak. The right fork goes on down to Hexum an the left fork goes to nowhere in partickaler. I'd never taken the left fork afor an allways had bin a mite cureeus bout jest where it did go. So I wander down it a piece a-fixin jest to go a little ways an then head on back. But the path is narra an tricksum an keeps on a-forkin off into smaller an smaller trails. For I know it, I am good an lost. Then, jest as I am bout to drop dead of sunstroke, I hear a crick a-rushin yonder. I fall down on my knees an thank Proveedance fer all that cool sweet water to drink. Then I spy a willer tree a-growin by the bank of the crick, an for you can say Jack Robinson, I'm a-snoozin neath her shadder.

An I dream of a house. Hits all red bricks an gray stones. The kind of house I might like to bild one of these days. A house full of doors an winders. An attic with gables an worms in the wood. An then, for I know it, I've spent all day up on cloud nine, an I wake up to see an ol graybeard a-standin over me. I reckon he's some kind of preecherman on account of the lawng black coat he's a-wearin deespite the blazin sun. He says to me, "I've bin expectin you, Jack!" an hands me a mason jar full of golden honey. There's not seed nor skin of my apples, so I set the jar in the basket in their place. It's eavnin now, an its all I can do to git on back home for dark.

Now my Ma she is awful surprized to see me bring home a mason jar full of honey stead of a few coppers like she was expectin. But stead of scoldin me an whuppin my backside like she shood a done, she brushes my hair with her speshal brush an makes me a cup of tea out of that thar honey.

The next day Ma wakes me up real early jest as the rooster is a-crowin COCKADOODLEOO. She gives me that mason jar full of honey an sends me off down to Hexum agin to see what I can fetch fer it. The jar of honey ain't near as hevvy as the basket full of apples had bin, an the road don't stretch on so lawng this time. When I git to the fork agin, I'm a-feelin a mite more advenchersum, an I reckon I'll see what's a-yonder that crick I found yesterday. The trail gits all thorny an full of brambles, an the britches of my overhalls are near bout tore up to shreds. Finely, I git myself to a soft litle brar patch an I am so eggzawsted from a-crawlin threw thorns an bramble that I fall fast asleep.

When I wake up agin this time it's to jingle-janglin, some crazy jingle-janglin. It's some fella all dressed up in black an white cloathes with bells on his wrists an ankles. His face is painted up like a girl, but I knows it's a man. He don't say a word, jest dances an makes funny faces at me. Then he snatches up my jar of honey an hands me a glass key in boot. Now this is a mite peculyer I thinks to myself. I wonder what in tarnation a glass key could go to. So I foller this jingle-jangly feller threw the bramble an he knows jest eggzackly where to step without a-gittin all tangled up in the thorn. But he's a-skippin so fast I cain't hardly keep up with him, an evencherly he pulls out of site. But I keep on a-followin in his footsteps till I come to a gate all made all out of glass.

Aha! I thinks to myself. The glass key must fit this here glass gate. An so it does, jest like a glove. Yonder the gate is a garden with walls all round an vines of ivy a-creepin down over the walls like a lacy spider web. All manner of flowers grow in this garden, an there are critters too like rabbits an possums an silver bells an cockleshells all in a row. An smack dab there in the middle is a waterin hole with three girls a-swimmin round in it without nary a stitch a cloathin on. An they say onto me, "A-come on in! The water's fine!" So I take off my cloathes an git in the waterin hole with em. They don't seem quite human, like they're pixies or sompin, on account of their skin is all green. So I ask em how come their skin is all green, an one of em takes my hand an pushes it into this spot in the ground under the water. I dig with my hand an green mud comes a-bubblin up out of the hole. The girls start a-smeerin it all over my body from head to toe till I am as green as an unripe tomater. Then I lie out in the sun fer a spell till the mud is all dried up an flakes right off of me. Then the pixies give me a gold ring an I follow a bunny rabbit all the way home.

When I show the ring to my Ma, she is all eggsited an jumps fer joy an whoops an hollers an says, "I knew it Jack. You're all growed up now. It's time you found yourself a wife."

Next mornin, I heer that old red rooster a-crowin like I never heerd him crow afor. Like the whole world is new. My Ma makes me a big old breakfast of bacon an eggs an pones an marmalade, an fixes up a pot of her finest China Orange tea which she pours into her best Devonshar teacups from out of the china closet.

She opens up a yellow pine wardrobe an pulls out a dandy black suit all lined with red silk. It's English from my daddy an it fits me jest like a glove. Then she takes a teensy little diemond key from out of her bosom an opens up a little cherrywood box. Inside it is a gold watch full of geers an springs a-wheelin around like stars an planets an she winds it up with a tiny gold key on the end of a chain which sets it a-tick-tick-tickin. Finely, she opens up a cedar box that she keeps by her bedside, an inside is a fancy silver key that looks jest as old as the hills. She says mind that key with extra speshal care on account of I'll need it to git into the house. So I pull on out of there to make my fortune. An Ma rings the bells in the church-house fer the first time in my whole life. *Jingle jangle. Travellin Jack never looked back.*

* * *

Onwards I go, a-trudgin along down the dry an dusty trail, past the fork, past the crick, past the bramble, past the garden till I find myself in wide-open newground. By this time I am a-boilin like a teakettle on a stove all done up in my dandy black suit. I shore am grateful fer all them cotton candy clouds a-rollin in over the sun. But for lawng, them clouds are all come over angry an grey, an I reckon I'd best look fer cover.

Jest then, the first drops of rain fall, a-drip-drip-drippin down. I spy an old barn over yonder in between two oak trees an I make fer it. The rain picks up, a-batterin down on my hat brim like little hammers, an I break into a mad dash. Neers I can reckon, this barn aint bin used in many lawng yeers on account of the rafters are all fallen in. All the better, I reckon, on account of there won't be no farmer in the mornin a-tellin me to scoot.

The rain is a-porin in threw all the holes in the roof, but I find me a nice patch of dry hay over in the corner to curl up an listen to the pixy shot a-clattrin on the roof an the wolf wind a-howlin threw the woods. I stand a rusty old pitchfork up on end an hang my daddy's English clothes on it to dry, a-wishin I had me a trusty set of overhalls to wear.

Come sunup I awake all covered in mornin dew. Nudged by a gentle finger of gold, my eyelids commence to fluttrin. I creep out of the hay an spread my arms out wide like a butterfly a-stretchin his wings. The barn looks jest like a house of cards that's a-fallen in. An I'm the Jack of spades, I reckon. I dress up in my daddy's English clothes agin—britches over legs, shirt over arms, scarf around neck, weskit over shirt an coat over weskit. Then I heers a rustlin in the barn. I grab the pitchfork an holler, "Who goes a-yonder?" Up pops a man all tatterd an torn. He is a-wearin nothin but shreds, an is a-hidin in the corner a-lookin at me with jackrabbit eyes. He says, "I kissed the maid. I kissed her it's true. She looked so forlorn I hadn't a clue."

So I say, "Don't be a-feered, I mean you no ill."

"An now I'm dead, I'm done I am. Down I go with eggs an ham . . ."

"Eggs an ham! Now yer talking."

". . . but if I pray an act real good, I might be saved by Robin Hood . . ."

". . . an maybe a big old pot of coffee . . ."

"Bowman."

". . . an toast with bosunberry jam . . ."

"At your service."

"Jack Drake at yours. Maybe tea stead of coffee."

"Jack in the Green. Jack with his hound an horn. Jack will have tea. Jack will have a cup. On the table down or up."

"Does he live far?"

"A hop a skip an a jump.

> "To Jack's house we go,
> To Jack's house we go;
> Heigh-ho, the derry-o,
> To Jack's house we go."

I shore am hongry on account of I ain't a had a lick to eat since I pulled out of my Ma's house yesterday mornin. I am a-tickled pink at the idear of tea an maybe some pones with bosunberry jam. An eggs an sawsedge? That'd be too good to be true. We step out of the barn into the brod daylight, the sun a-floatin up there in the sky like a great big yellow egg yoke, an the light is a-stabbin my eyes like a jack knife. The farm is a grizzly site—waggon wheels an ploughshares a-layin in the mud, rusty arn sickles an spades an shovels. In the stable is the skeleton of a dead hoss still a-wearin a bridle an rains. A sceercrow in a raggedy coat is a-standin at the garden wall, straw head grinnin like a madcap, two jackdaws perched one on each sholeder. I reckon he's king of all he sees—this land of bones an shovels. It is a grewsum site to be shore.

I'm a-rarin to see what's inside the house. Maybe some tea an vittles. But Bowman says it's all locked up, an he's a-feered to go inside. So I says, "Can't be more feersum than what's on the outside." I sidles up to the front door, all solid oak it is, with a lion's head carved in it, a brass ring danglin from the mouth. Jest fer kicks I knock on the door with the brass ring *tap-tap-tap* an wait to see if a body answers. But all I heer is my tappin echoin round inside the empty house.

Then I recollect the silver key my Ma gave me, an a-wonder if maybe—naw that'd be too good to be true—but I try it jest the same. An I declare! Shore nuff it slips right into that keyhole *clickedy-clack* an the door swings wide open. An I think to myself cureeus, sir. Cureeus. Yonder the door I see a lawng hall with a mahogany floor an walls decked with pitchers of ladies an gennlemen from lawng ago. At the end of the hall is a stair case with a crooked rail. Off to the right of the hall is a settin room with velvet couches an fancy footstools, an to the left is a dinin room with a polished table long enough to set an army. An a deelux shandeleer is a-hangin from the seelin.

At the head of the table is a big old oak chair all carved with creepin vines of ivy an little angels with wings. An on the wall behind the throne is a great arn shield a-painted with a feerse blood-red dragon with two legs a-standin proud.

So I set myself down on the chair jest fer fun an puff my fethers up. Bowman bends his knee to me an sets at my right hand. My squar. Quite so, I thinks to myself. But the table is bares Old Mother Hubbard's cubbard. We shood be eatin breakfast by now. Well, I reckon where there's a dinin room, there ought to be a kitchen somewhere. An shore nuff there is! An where there's a kitchen, there's a pantry. An where there's a pantry, there's a cubbard. An glory be! I find a tin of deelishus China Orange tea. Smells like breakfast.

So we make ourselves at home a-choppin wood fer the stove, a-fetchin water fer the kettle, an a-pickin berries fer vittles. No biskits though or we wood a made jam out of them berries. But there's some real fine china in the china closet, silver spoons an all, with little D's on em. We have ourselves a ball a-drinkin tea an eatin berries at that lawng table jest like nights of old. I gits to thinking this must be how my daddy lived way back in Merry Old England. May be I was really Sir Jack or sompin.

After tea we are a-settin in the den layin back in velvet couches a-smokin a plug of baccy I got out of my hip pocket. An I gits to wondrin what's at the top of that stair case with the crooked rail. Bowman dozn't think we ought to go up there on account of them stairs are so old we could fall plum threw. An I says, "I thought we were nights of old, the kind that whupped dragons an suchlike. I shore ain't a-feared of no rickety stairs." An without hesertatin, I mount em one foot up an the other foot down, the stairs a-creekin below me.

Round about halfway up the creekin gets awful loud, an I reckon maybe this warn't such a good idear after all. I grab onto the crooked railin an it snaps right off in my hand, dowels a-flyin ever which way. Jest as I am about to teeter over the side, I feel two arms wrop round my sholeders an pull me back from the brink.

"Ah Bowman, you are a goodly squar to be shore. I reckon fools rush in where angels are a-feered to tred."

So we climb on up the rest of the stairs like a couple of jokers till we gits to the top where we find to a door at the end of a hall. It's a black wood door with a silver doorknob shaped like an acorn.

Tender as a lamb, I turn that silver doorknob an open the door jest a crack so I can poke my head in fer a peek. A-yonder is a rat-crawlin attic, dark an musty with yeers of dust on the floor, the walls a-covered in cobwebs, the eeves full of day-dreamin bats.

In the corner is an old trunk an inside the trunk is a worm-eaten book, a brass bell an a candlestub. I set myself down on the floor, an strikin my last match on my daddy's English heel, light the candlestub. Then I gits to reedin the book while Bowman bides at the door.

>The old church stood in spite of wood
>   Fair riddled through with worms;
>Y^e Shepherd's beard was snowy white,
>   His eyes as grey as storms.
>
>Three daughters did Y^e Shepherd have,
>   Fair skinned and light of hair,
>Sweet Daisy was the youngest one;
>   Her face was passing fair.
>
>When Daisy was a little girl,
>   She kept herself in shade;
>She found no solace in the sun,
>   A wistful sighing maid.
>
>Y^e Shepherd lingered at the door
>   Until his girls came in.
>He called them at the stroke of four,
>   To save their souls from sin.
>
>But Daisy would not come to tea;
>   She crept into her room—

A cobweb-shrouded darkling place,
    Neglected by the broom.

Beneath her bed, a cedar chest,
    Her mother's quilt inside—
A garden full of memories,
    Which in her mind had died.

She wrapped herself inside the quilt,
    Although it smelt of mold,
And dreamt of times before her birth,
    Of stories she was told.

Lord Ettinfell lived long ago,
    A curse upon his name.
The House of Drake and built by Jack,
    Were both one and the same.

Beneath the moon the Drakes took tea,
    Long steeped with honey'd yew.
The Tea of Dreams the cup was called;
    It was a witch's brew.

In John Drake's dreams a truelove called,
    A vision in the dark.
And like his fathers all before
    To her did he embark.

The next day Drake set out to ride,
    And suitably he dressed—

Red riding coat and silken hose;
    He always wore his best.

He paid respect as Drakes must do,
    To Oake and Ashe and Thorne,
A custom that was recognised
    From long ere he was born.

His Yeoman riding next to him,
    Drake came to Hexham Town,
Where there were many whisperings,
    For he had dark renown.

Where two roads met Drake came upon
    A man dressed all in black;
It was the self-same tattered wretch
    Who'd damned his sire Jack.

'Well met, my lord,' said Mr. Scratch.
    'You wear a costly coat.
Such garments are unknown to me,
    To such a lowly goat.

'We'll meet again, of that I'm sure,
    Or my name isn't Scratch.
Our fates are like a truelove knot,
    Their threads a perfect match.'

The next day Drake a greybeard met
    Who on a fiddle play'd.

And in return for bread he ate,
    An ancient riddle say'd:

'I start my life upon a forge;
    My other half conjoins.
To turn my tongue may thus disgorge
    A hidden cache of coins.'

That night Drake lay in Devon grass;
    His Yeoman broke their trust
To steal a taste of Dreaming Tea,
    A few drops all he dust.

He dreamt his master hied his horse,
    A horn clutched in his hand,
And blew a call to heavens high,
    Which echo'd 'cross the land.

The scarlet-coated hunter fell
    Upon the cold black earth;
The fox he hunted on him set
    And tore his throat with mirth.

John Drake awoke in perfect peace,
    The day about to start;
His Yeoman had no words for him,
    A secret in his heart.

Upon the seventh day of Yule,
    Drake rode to Cornish heath

To dream within the standing stones
    Around him like a wreath.

Three further days of Yuletide passed,
    While Drake in cold grass slept;
And on the fourth, come breaking dawn,
    From out of shadows crept

Old Scratch, the devil—both the same—
    To offer him a deal.
And there Drake clasped Old Scratch's hand,
    His wedding day to seal.

And on the final day of Yule,
    Two Englishmen set sail;
On canvas wings they swiftly flew
    For fair winds did prevail.

They set their feet in younger land,
    A teeming sailors' port,
Where dark corsairs flashed ill-got wares
    To women who made sport.

A fiddler's son the tavern played,
    His name was Frankie Dew;
He scraped to court a single girl—
    To her his heart was true.

A Scot with but a single eye
    Wassailed Drake with a verse,

An ancient rhyme that could be thought
    A blessing or a curse.

'I wolf sweet words, the songs of man,
    And yet no letters know;
For all the knowledge I take in,
    I never wiser grow.'

In cutting through this twisty knot,
    A master-stroke Drake made;
The answer was the wriggling worm
    That mouldered books invade.

'A cunning man you are for sure;
    Well, Logan is my name.
I'll take you west to join Y^e Tribe;
    Our paths are both the same.'

Into the hills the three men struck,
    Where dwelt Y^e Tribe of Weird.
Three Sisters sat beneath a tree
    And what they wove was feared.

On Easter morn a feast was held
    To seal Drake to Y^e Tribe;
His arms were sewn into a quilt,
    And noted by a scribe.

The Sisters bade him steep his Tea
    With blood drawn by a thorn;

> He shot an arrow in the air,
>   And so his weird was born.
>
> O woe O woe White Shepherd's dead,
>   An arrow through his heart;
> A raven perched upon his head,
>   A witness to black art.
>
> Wan Daisy then and Drake were wed,
>   To Yeoman's stark dismay,
> And dead the Drake lay on her bed;
>   I sing to rue the day.
>
> Hear how was born Y^e Shepherd Black
>   I curse the day—alack!
> And pray be crushed beneath the heel
>   Of time's relentless wheel.

As I am a-reedin, the words take on a life of their own, with bug eyes starin back at me from the a's an o's an feelers a-wigglin off the g's an q's. I can't tell if I'm a-reedin the words or if they are a-reedin me. Then a sickly groan comes from under the floor. It sounds like the stirrin of some slombrin beast. Bowman, who was quiet as a mouse while I was a-reedin the book, commences to hollerin, "The house is a-fallin! The house is a-fallin!" Shore nuff I hear the crackin of wood an then a *kee-rash!* A beam falls an smashes all that china we done laid out on the table downstairs. The house is a-fallin jest like London Bridges. I spook an run back to the stairs, but they're a-fallin too. Then Bowman says, "Lookit the seelin!" I look up an glory be there's a round door in the seelin with a brass doorknob smack dab in the middle of it like the sun up in the sky. Bowman gives me a leg up an I try to open it. It's locked. My hopes are dashed. An then I recollect the tiny gold key at the end of my watch chain. It fits jest like a glove in little bitty keyhole next to the doorknob. *Click.* I swing the door open an scramble up threw it. Bowman passes me up the candle, an I reach down an grab his hand jest as the floor gives way. An with all my might I pull him up from the pit, a-flailin the bell behind him *ding-a-ling ding*. I find a rusty old lantern an put the candle inside it. In the flickrin light I see a spiral stair a-windin up above us. Our Jacob's ladder to salvashun. We climb the stairs up into a garret which is still standin somehow even though the rest of the house is a-fallen in.

Wropt up in a mill-dewed swatch of black wool is a skeleton a-slumped over a book on an ink-stayned writin desk, a goose fether still stuck in his finger bones. At the skeleton's feet is a clay jug. I wonder if whatever was in it is what made him write so long he up an died a-doin it. I take a little sip of the contents of the jug, jest the teeniest tiniest drop on the tip of my tung, but it's enough to spred like wildfar. That is some angry hunny, but sweet as nectar. I pick the book up off the writin desk an set down in a chair with purple pillows next to a window where the moonlight comes a-streemin in. Bowman is plum tuckerd an falls right to sleep a-curled up in a corner of the room. That suits me fine an I commence to reedin the book while the House of Drake comes a-fallin down, fallin down, my fair lady.

Childe Jackson Drake

– III –
The Lay of Jackson Drake

Childe Jackson to the dark house came,
    The house in Shepherd's Wood.
His beldam's sires had borne that name;
    As long as it had stood.

He journey'd far to Shepherd's House,
    A Key upon a chain,
An heirloom from his grandmother,
    His kindred's secret bane.

Ten ravens perched upon the roof,
    A gable for their nest,
And at the door, an owl beseech'd,
    'Who are you? What's your quest?'

'Why, I am Drake, the son of Jack,
    Just journeyed up the dell.
I seek Y^e Olde, Y^e Shepherd Black,
    To save my soul from Hell.'

The Owl watched him with glowing eyes
    That in the darkness see.
'If you are of the blood of Jack,
    Then you will have a Key.'

So Drake produced Y^e Silver Key,
    Which fit into the door,
And strode into the Shepherd's House,
    Boots tapping on the floor.

The ebon hall in Shepherd's House
    Was dark and wide and cold.
Its denizen lived all alone,
    And some called him Y^e Olde.

'I am Y^e Olde, Y^e Shepherd Black,
    An Angell for a dam;
I welcome Drake, the son of Jack,
    For I your cousin am.

'The Sisters Wyrd are much a-feared,
    For Madness bubbles up.
Black horsemen ride with beasts astride
    Unless you win Y^e Cup.

'Y^e White Cup lies beyond Nine Gates,
    To which there are Nine Keys.
I'll give you these Nine Keys to Hell,
    The Sistren to appease.

'But in return, I ask a price,
    The Emerald in Y^e Cup.
Bring it to me, my cousin dear,
    Or Hell will eat you up.'

Then screech'd Y ᵉ Owl: 'The deal is done!'
 And Jackson turned the Key
That opened up the Gate of Time,
 A door where none should be.

He crossed the Gate into a reed,
 Which hid the House of Hare;
A roof of straw and walls of sod:
 It was a cozy lair.

'Well met,' declared Yᵉ Rampant Hare.
 'I'll pour us tea for two;
I'll lead you to the Second Gate;
 A debt will then be due.

'To blackest Hell I'll lead you sure;
 From you I have one need:
A patch behind your noble house
 To overgrow with weed.'

So Jackson and Yᵉ Rampant Hare
 Set out to find the HWOL;
They saw it in a murky pond
 Behind a secret knoll.

A water sprite dwelt in the pond,
 As happy as could be.
'I'll carry you into the HWOL
 If you will marry me.'

While Lily swam into the dark,
    Drake clutched fast to her skin.
And down he went, down far below;
    The Second Key went in.

'Your steel is strong, my courtly knight,
    But stronger still the sheath.
So kiss me long into the night,
    And hold me underneath.'

A White Horse shod with golden shoes
    The next morn Drake did find.
His canter did Y^e Childe amuse—
    A tail that swished behind.

'You need a steed, my courtly knight,
    So climb up on my back,
And into Hell shall we take flight,
    O noble son of Jack.

'And all I ask of you in turn,
    A stable snug and warm.'
'The deal is done,' declared Y^e Owl.
    They charged into the storm.

And down the muddy road he rode,
    The sullen son of Jack,
Until he reached the Stygian bridge
    From which may none turn back.

And there he found a Monkey bound,
    Who shook his chains and cried,
'A Silver Key will set me free,
    My hope has never died.'

So Jackson loosed the Monkey's chains,
    And opened up a Gate.
He broke the bonds which tie us all,
    And make men mock and hate.

Across the bridge there stopped a train;
    Drake boarded it to ride.
He found a berth for Lily's bed,
    And lay himself beside.

The grim conductor rattled chains,
    And had a skull-like head.
His body but a bag of bones,
    He looked like he was dead.

'I ask of you my riddle's key,
    And I have naught to hide;
Your answer will your ticket be,
    And pay me for your ride.

'O what is higher than a tree,
    And heavier than lead,
And what is deeper than the sea,
    And tastier than bread?

'And what is whiter than the milk,
    And sharper than a thorn,
And what is softer than the silk,
    And louder than a horn?'

And Jackson turned a Key to Hell
    By how he made reply.
There was no sharper wit than he;
    The son of Jack was sly.

'O heaven's higher than a tree,
    And sin outweighs the lead,
And Hell is deeper than the sea,
    And blessing outsweets bread.

'And snow is whiter than the milk,
    And hunger outpricks thorn,
And down is softer than the silk,
    And shame the loudest horn.'

The train then left them in a town
    Called Tupelo by name;
Some say that there a king was born,
    A beggar all the same.

The rain fell down in Tupelo,
    No welcome for them there,
No pillow for poor Jackson's head,
    Or Lily or Y^e Hare.

No tavern's warmth or food or drink,
    And jailed for vagrancy,
The monkey sprung them from the clink;
    He jacked the sheriff's key.

Right quick they then flew out of town,
    The sheriff on their trail;
The Duke boys hid them in a barn,
    And gave them beds and ale.

The rooster crowed the crack of dawn,
    And coffee Drake was served;
He relished long his eggs and ham,
    A breakfast well deserved.

Drake saddled up his sturdy horse,
    And galloped out of town;
He did his best to stay the course
    While rain came pouring down.

And down the road a carny came;
    A barker ran his mouth.
'Folks, come and see the spectacle!
    The Wonder of the South.

'See He-She-It arrayed in chains,
    A horned three-headed freak,
A giant from a fairy tale—
    You'll want to take a peek.

'Here liontamers, girls with beards
    And oddities abound.
All tickets are a dollar, folks,
    The cheapest show around.'

Then by a shoestring puppet show,
    Childe Jackson met a girl.
She read his fortune with her cards,
    Which made his fate unfurl.

His path was forked so said her cards,
    A spade on ev'ry one;
His father took the crooked path,
    So straight must walk the son.

The rope which held the bigtop up,
    Was bound up in a knot
As twisted as a wyvern's tail;
    Untie it Drake could not.

And Satan said, 'Who will untie
    My twisty little snag?'
His mouth was twisted in a smile,
    That arch beguiling wag.

The Fifth Key turned into a sword
    To cleave the knot in two,
So Satan ran, his purpose spurned;
    And back to Hell he flew.

That tent of blue they call the sky
    Then came a-tumbling down;
A bat from hell, the carny flew,
    Packed up and skipped the town.

A cockatrice, or basilisk,
    Is hatched from basest dung,
And if you catch the merest glance
    Your death knell will be rung.

A Billy Goat with flashing eyes
    Asked Drake a deal be done.
'I'll carry you across the wall
    If you give me a son.'

'I'd scale that wall better'n no goat,'
    The White Horse blurted out.
'Don't take that deal; climb on my back;
    That bargain I will flout.'

The Monkey caught yon Lurker's eye,
    Averting so its gaze.
The White Horse then climbed up the wall;
    His skill did all amaze.

He kicked the monster with his hooves;
    Y^e Lurker then fell down,
Like Humpty Dumpty from the wall,
    Its screams alarmed the town.

The Cockatrice cracked like an egg,
    Its binding rune thus broke,
And as it shattered into bits,
    The Sixth Gate so awoke.

Childe Jackson went whence none return,
    Where Lucifer await,
Y^e Lake of Fire where sinners burn,
    Before him yawned the Gate.

A Court of Crows assembled there,
    Asmodeus the Judge,
And Lucifer the Litigant,
    Who held an age-old grudge.

A Boar defended Jackson Drake,
    And ah, now here's the rub:
The prosecutor was the Goat,
    Still smarting from the snub.

'All hear! All hear!' the Judge declared.
    'The trial has now begun.
How do you plead Childe Jackson Drake,
    Whom Jack once called a son?'

'A word of counsel,' said the Boar.
    'A truth that I have learned.
Whatever that is said in Court
    Against you can be turned.'

'How do you plead?' the Judge enquired.
    'To deals thy father struck?'
'I shall not pay for inborn sin,'
    Said Drake to push his luck.

'Irrelevant,' the Goat replied,
    His tone a haughty sneer.
'That Jack is bound and so his son,
    The terms are crystal-clear.'

'Then who stands Witness,' asked the Judge.
    'To damn the Drake to Hell?'
And into Court an Angel flew,
    Whose name was Azazel.

He quoth, 'I will. I saw the deed.
    I witnessed well the deal.
Jack signed his name with blood and quill,
    And so his fate did seal.'

Then sauntered in a gold-haired Prince,
    Lord Lucifer by name,
Who fell from grace and ever since
    Has played a double game.

The court all rose for their fair King,
    Whose locks streamed long behind;
Black ravens from their perch took wing,
    Magnificent in kind.

The Dæmon Prince a watch then drew
    From out of his silk vest;
The wheel of time did sorely put
    His patience to the test.

He placed a hand upon a book,
    And took the Oath of Wyrms:
'The truth and lies are both the same,
    And naught my oath confirms.'

The Billy Goat did snort and champ.
    'My client stakes his claim
To take the soul of Jackson Drake
    As Jack he did the same.'

Y^e Buke of Olde is bound in skin,
    Where all of Time is found;
Two cherubim did crack it wide,
    And in it Jack was bound.

'Fear not the deal, my dearest son;
    I have your freedom here.
Your drink from Y^e White Cup is won;
    Of Hell you have no fear.'

The cherubs closed Y^e Olden Buke,
    And in the Court did land
A seraph decked with beryl rings,
    A letter in his hand.

'To Jackson Drake I offer you
    A drink from my White Cup
If you will come to me tonight
    And join me in my sup.'

'The deal is done,' then screech'd Y^e Owl;
    A reckoning was due.
The Seventh Gate swung open wide
    For Jackson to pass through.

A soaring stair he found therein;
    It spiralled up and up.
He climbed it till he huffed and puffed,
    A-thirsting for Y^e Cup.

Atop the stair an ashen door,
    As high as seven men.
He turned the Eighth Key in the lock;
    It opened for him then.

Queen Lilith lay upon a bed,
    A postered nest for one.
It was a rosy silken throne,
    And he a Night had won.

The Queen set tea for Jackson Drake,
    A pot of tea for two,
In china cups with silver spoons,
    And honey in them too.

As Jackson quaffed his cup of tea,
    Still reeling from the stairs;
He did not know until he had
    The state of his affairs.

A gust of wind so blew the Drake
    Up from Y^e Mouth of Hell;
Disgorged then by the final Gate,
    He climbed up from a well.

He brushed the dust then off his tails,
    The ash and soot and sand;
He found a stone, the Emerald,
    A-glitt'ring in his hand.

He drank an ale then at the inn
    That stood by crossing roads,
And left before the nighttime fell
    When drunkards crooned their odes.

He paid his due to Oake and Ashe,
    Without forgetting Thorne;
And sighting home the heavens heard
    Tantivy from his horn.

And in the hall a fire burned,
    Awaiting him Y^e Hare;
They roasted chestnuts in the fire,
    And all was well in there.

*
* * *
*

Yᵉ Buke of Olde

Debts	Due for	Due to
1 emerald	Nine Keys	Yᵉ Black Shepherd
1 patch of garden	Path to HWOL	Yᵉ Rampant Hare
1 conjugal bed	Yᵉ HWOL	Yᵉ Melusine
1 stable	Use of a Steed	Yᵉ White Horse
1 fare	Yᵉ Riddle	Yᵉ Conductor
1 tankard of ale	Court Costs	Yᵉ Contrary Boar
One Night	Yᵉ White Cup	Lilith

Old Effinfell, the House of Drake

– IV –
The Dream Emerald

Old Ettinfell, the sprawling House of Drake, lay past the river's bend, just north of Hexham Town. After harrowing the Nine Gates of Hell, Jackson Drake settled there with his wife Lily, who bore him three children: Gabriel, Josiah, and golden-curled Mary.

Behind the house was a green garden where Mary loved to play. Mary's favourite spot was an old rock, worn smooth by rain, where she would sit and hold court over a little pond. The pond was a tapestry of lily-pads, and on each lily-pad there sat a frog. The frogs would jump over one another like chess pieces, so it seemed to her, all at her command. And hither and yon flit the dragonfly, bearing messages to the throne of the queen. Good Queen Mary.

One day towards the end of March, just after the first robin redbreast had braved the saturnine oak which stood by the side of the house, the Rampant Hare came to visit Mary on her stone and invited her to come share some parsnip tea with him in the Yellow'd Reed. Mary was delighted and eagerly accepted, for she had never been invited into the Yellow'd Reed before.

The Rampant Hare threaded Mary through a winding footpath, bidding her be careful lest she become lost in the Reed. In the midst of the Yellow'd Reed was a tangled path of briar, and in the briar there grew a single white rose.

"O, what a pretty rose!" exclaimed Mary, who had never seen a rose quite so white before.

"Well come and have some tea," said the Rampant Hare. "And perhaps later I shall let you pluck it." The Rampant Hare set one cup, and then two cups, and then three.

"Who is the third cup for?" asked Mary.

The Rampant Hare stroked his whiskers with a furry paw and said, "Let's just say that I am expecting company—most esteemed company indeed. But let's begin without her." And he poured tea into two of the cups. Just then a hummingbird flew down and hovered gracefully over the white rose.

"Punctual as ever," commented the Rampant Hare, as he poured her a cup.

"Why, thank you, darling," purred the hummingbird, who all of a sudden turned into a beautiful lady with a green gown and cowslips in her hair.

"Mary, meet Sabrina," introduced the Rampant Hare courteously.

"Charmed, I'm sure," expected Sabrina, graciously extending a green-gloved hand.

"H-h-how do you?" dithered Mary, for she could scarcely believe her eyes.

"Be not afraid," said Sabrina. "I shan't bite you. Not yet anyway. Come and bring me my tea. I am thirsty after my long flight. Come, come, step where I tell you and you won't be tangled in the briar. Put your left foot a little to the right—very good. Tippy-toe with your right foot—gently now. Step over the root—carefully—with your left foot. Excellent! There now, that wasn't so bad, was it? Do you like the pretty white rose? Of course you do. Now pluck it, there's a good girl. Grab it by the stem and pull it out of the ground. Oh dear, did you prick your thumb with the thorn? How dreadful! It is nothing, just a little drop of blood spilt. But you must be tired. Sleep now. Here is a quiet spot for you to curl up in, right in the middle of the briar. Clutch the rose to your breast, and may it soothe you. There. Sleep now, Mary. Sleep . . ."

* * *

Nine ravens had come to roost in the gables over Ettinfell Hall. On the tenth gable was perched an old King Raven who proudly puffed his ebony livery. The King Raven bore a message for Jackson Drake clasped in his talon, a crimson envelope sealed with argent tallow and stamped with a fox's head, the mark of the Black Shepherd. Jackson accepted the letter with trembling hand and retreated to read it in the library.

> Y^e Ebon. Shep'd
> Dark End Wood
>
> My dear Jacksonne,
>
> Your debt to me is long overdue;
> My Word is the Law
> Be nothing else true.
>
> —S.

Jackson knew he had to settle accounts. He didn't know why he had tarried so long. He fished the key out from the locket he wore around his neck. The Diamond Key. The Key to the Ninth Gate. He slipped the key in the lock of the top left-hand drawer of his writing-desk. *Click.* He turned the lock twice to the left, once to the right. He opened the mahogany drawer. Inside the drawer was a cedar box, which was sealed by a binding spell known only to him. Jackson crossed his arms on his chest and uttered the Sacred Word, which lifted the spell.

He opened the box and beheld the Emerald in all its glittering glory, as each splendid facet snared a ray of candlelight and wove it into a radiant web of fire. Then he hissed the hated EDOM and closed the box again, locking it in the mahogany drawer with the Diamond Key.

* * *

IV. THE DREAM EMERALD

Mary was conspicuously absent from tea that afternoon. The Rampant Hare served tea to those present—Jackson, Lily, Gabriel, and Josiah. Lily, as usual, declined the scones, preferring instead to dine in private.

It was a morose tea, the silence broken only by the babbling brook which rushed from spout to cup, spout to cup, spout to cup, spout to cup, and then five piercing chimes of a silver clock. A dragonfly flew in through the window and perched atop Mary's vacant chair. The Rampant Hare poured her a cup.

"Mary lies sleeping," said the dragonfly. "Sleeping in the briar. Enchanted she was by a servant of the Black Shepherd. I am willing to lead an envoy as far as the Deep Blue Sea to bring the Emerald to Dark End Wood. Who will come with me and carry the stone?"

Jackson glanced nostalgically at the sword which was mounted on the wall, all dusty and covered with cobwebs.

"Alas," he sighed, "I have dawdled too many a year, and now am too old to make good the bargain I struck with the Black Shepherd."

"I shall carry it," blurted Gabriel, who brashly took up his father's arms from the wall.

"No, you shall carry the sword," seconded Josiah wisely. "Because you are as bold as brass. But I shall bear the Emerald, for I know how to hide in secret places." The deal was done.

"I shall sew a sack for each of you," promised Lily. "With a needle of rat's bone and a thread of cat's gut, I shall sew them tonight at the witching hour."

"And I shall saddle up two worthy steeds from the stable," offered the Rampant Hare, bowing. "I'll feed them oats and corn. They'll be ready to ride at daybreak."

"So be it," said Jackson Drake. "Come to my library in the morning. Come before the cock crows." He took his cup and retired for the night.

* * *

The eastern sky was tinged with a crimson glow, a whisper of which suffused the dismal sanctum where Jackson Drake met with his two sons that fateful morning. Gabriel and Josiah were already fully dressed in riding coats and breeches, and Jackson wore the azure dressing gown, which was his habit when he immersed himself in his books.

He handed each of his sons a jingling bag of gold to cover their expenses. To Gabriel he bestowed a bottle of Berserker Potion, which when drunk would send him into a blood fury and make him indomitable in battle. To Josiah he proffered *The Book of Norn*, full of ancient wisdom to counsel them in times of confusion. Then he opened the mahogany drawer with the Diamond Key and turned the cedar box over to Josiah's hands.

"Within this box is kept an Emerald," he said. "The box has no lock but must not be opened without uttering the Sacred Word. What word this is need not concern you, for the Black Shepherd will know it, and you must deliver the box unopened."

At that moment the cock crowed and a golden shaft of sunlight penetrated the room.

"Be off then," croaked Jackson, shielding his eyes from the unaccustomed light as he drew the curtains. "May the Blessings of Woden be on your brows, and the Winds of the Wyrd at your backs."

Gabriel and Josiah kissed their father's cheeks and left the library just as the crows were beginning to caw.

* * *

Lily set an English breakfast for her two children: two eggs with bacon, China tea in a silver pot (with lemon), and plenty of buttered toast and jam. Fighting to keep her composure, she presented Gabriel and Josiah with the sacks she had sewn, amply furnished with buckles and buttons and pockets, inside and out.

"If ever you find yourselves cold or hungry," she told them. "Or in sickness or want of comfort, reach into your bag and let your fingers find what you need." The children solemnly accepted their mother's gifts.

"You need not be worried," boasted Gabriel. "For we shall return triumphant."

"Set tea for us a year from this day," asked Josiah. "And if we have not returned, you need never set it for us again."

IV. THE DREAM EMERALD

"I shall set places for you every day until that time," promised Lily. "Now get along with you, afore I bust out in tears . . ."

The Rampant Hare had saddled two of the finest steeds from the stable for Gabriel and Josiah—Sleipnir for Gabriel and Hrimfaxi for Josiah. Both were scions of the White Horse which had charged their father into Pandaemonium. He had sharpened Kaliburn for Gabriel, and to Josiah he presented his own blade, Chrysaor, which was said to have belonged to Artegall himself. Dragonfly was waiting for them, hovering by the stable door.

The brothers mounted their horses, slipping boots into stirrups and prodding spurs into flanks. "Gee up!" they cried, and they were off. A robin redbreast watched them from the highest branch of the saturnine oak and began to sing . . .

* * *

The brothers rode, the brothers rode, and the brothers rode some more, down the crooked mile, up the hill, and over the dale, over sun-dappled meadows, across rain-swollen rivers, around snow-covered mountains, and under rainbow-splendoured skies. At last, as the lingering salmon traces of twilight began to wane, and their horses began to sag under the weight of their saddles, the brothers stopped. They had come to the end of a dead road and wondered if the dragonfly had led them astray. But the dragonfly would not say a peep and alighted on a maple branch, falling fast asleep.

Gabriel gathered a pile of wood, and Josiah laid out a circle of stones. They got a good little fire going, about which they huddled, shivering as much from fear as from the cold, for they had never been so far from home before. The moon was a slender crescent and hung like a reaper's scythe above the mountains to the west. It was then that Josiah suggested that they reach into one of their sacks for something to comfort them. So Gabriel unbuckled his sack and rummaged around it until he found some pipes. He put them to his lips and, after blowing a few tentative notes, began to play a song. Josiah joined in, singing the words:

> *"There were three men come out of the west,*
>
> *Their fortunes for to try.*
>
> *And these three men made a solemn vow,*
>
> *John Barleycorn must die . . ."*

Just then a twig snapped. Gabriel put down his pipe, and Josiah reached for his sword. They peered into the bushes where they had heard the sound and saw a rustling in the underbrush.

"Who goes there?" demanded Gabriel. "Friend or foe?" A hatless head popped out of the bush.

"'Tis but I, Tom Truepenny," came the quavering reply. "I mean no harm. I have but lost my way."

"Then come and join us by the fire," offered Josiah.

"Oh, thank 'ee, sir. Thank 'ee kinely." A sprightly little imp sprang over to their campsite. He was a grimy boy, hardly thirteen, and his clothes were but tattered shreds of canvas. Josiah handed him a slice of cheese, which he snatched eagerly and gobbled down in one bite. After he had sated his appetite, Tom Truepenny told his tale.

"My father was an honest soul, and he owned a grocery near Land's End. He was not a wealthy man, but he earned enough coppers to pay the rent every quarter and put supper on the table at night. After supper, when we were sitting by the fire and all the world was drowsing, sometimes my father would light his long-stemmed pipe and tell stories to us chil'en. He would tell us stories about Jack, who came from Cornwall as we did, and left his country to become a giant-killer. My father's stories filled my head with notions, and I decided that I too would leave home to slay giants like Jack. So one night I put some cakes in my pockets and ran away from home whilst my father was sleeping. I have wandered lost for many days now, my cakes have run out, and I have had to forage in the wood for roots and berries to eat."

The brothers gave their hands in friendship to Tom and told him of their quest. They invited him to join them on the their journey to bring the Emerald to the Black Shepherd, an offer which Tom accepted eagerly, for the quest was much like one of his father's stories. The clouds broke, and the stars glittered overhead. Gabriel struck up the pipes, and together the three finished the song which two had begun.

> "Here's little Sir John in a nut-brown bowl,
> And brandy in a glass,
> And little Sir John in a nut-brown bowl
> Proved the strongest man at last,
>
> "For the huntsman he can't hunt the fox,
> Nor loudly blow his horn,
> And the tinker can't mend kettles or pots
> Without a little of the Barleycorn!"

The next morning they awoke early as the first orange shafts of sunlight were climbing over the mountains to the east. Making tea from the mint leaves which grew by their campsite, Gabriel and Josiah found some scones in their sacks, which they shared with Tom.

The dragonfly was anxious to depart, having risen before the sun and breakfasted on some juicy grubs. Tom climbed up into Gabriel's saddle and they began to ride. The dragonfly led them down the Path of Forever May, which was very narrow, and they had to ride one by one. The Path of Forever May was all overgrown with flowers of every colour, and they soon found themselves covered from head to toe with pollen. Tom began to sneeze. At noon they stopped by a babbling brook for a drink and a splash, and by mid-afternoon they had reached the end of the Path of Forever May, which led to the Ruined Garden.

The Ruined Garden was enclosed by a rusty wrought-iron fence whose gate squeaked at the hinges. Creeping vines clung to the fence, and all manner of weeds grew here. In the middle of the garden was a stone fountain, full of rainwater, and its sides were covered with moss. They dismounted and sat under the shadow of an ancient oak, like the one which stood next to Old Ettinfell.

A grey squirrel darted onto of the branches of the tree and introduced himself:

"I am Gnarlatosk, at your service. Would you be looking for a knothole? That is the business of most who come to the Ruined Garden."

"Aye, that we would," replied Josiah, though he had not a clue as to what a knothole was.

"Well, if you would be so kind as to lend a hand and help me gather up some acorns, I might be persuaded to show you one."

So they helped the grey squirrel gather up acorns, until a substantial pile had been heaped up in front of the tree.

"I am very grateful," said the Gnarlatosk. "The knothole, of course, lies in the trunk of the oak. Up by that branch there. Which one of you will climb the tree with me?"

"I will," volunteered Tom. "For I am very nimble, and good at climbing trees." So Tom grabbed hold of one of the lower branches and scrambled up the oak after the grey squirrel, who flashed up the trunk quick as lightning. Huffing and puffing, he reached the branch where the squirrel sat waiting impatiently. And sure enough, there was the knothole. Gnarlatosk disappeared into the hole, and Tom followed after. The knothole was small, but big enough for Tom to squeeze through. Shuddering at the bugs, he crawled a good little way through the tiny aperture until he came to a little chamber, hardly bigger than a closet. Slowly his eyes adjusted to the dim greenish light, which had no apparent source, and Tom realized that he was standing at the top of a spiral stair that wound down further than he could see.

The grey squirrel had already scampered down the stair, and Tom wondered whether he should go back and tell his friends what he had found or venture down by himself. Perhaps he would go just a little ways.

The stairs, which were made of marble, descended into a dream pit. There was sixty-six stairs in all. Reaching the foot of the stair, Tom found himself standing before three gates, of which only the middle one was open. The other two were locked up as tight as a drum. He cautiously stepped through the open gate, which led to a long tunnel. A cold wind blew through the tunnel and Tom shivered.

IV. THE DREAM EMERALD

He walked down the tunnel until he came to a juncture. The tunnel split into two: one to the left, and one to the right. Tom could already tell that this adventure was going to get hairy, so he reached into his pocket and pulled out one of the bundle of acorns he had stashed and left it there to mark his trail. Then he flipped a penny to choose which tunnel to go down: heads the right one, tails the left. The penny came up heads.

This tunnel led to a three-way juncture. Tom was beginning to wish he had gone back for Gabriel and Josiah. But he had made his bed. He left another acorn and started down the middle tunnel.

This tunnel wound like a snake, curving to the left and curving to the right until it came to a door. The door was tall and imposing and had a brass ring set in the dead centre. Tom pulled on the ring, and to his surprise the door swung open with no trouble. Inside the door was an empty chamber about twenty feet wide, twenty feet long, and twenty feet high. The chamber had stone walls, a stone ceiling, and a stone floor. Disappointed that his efforts had yielded only an empty room, Tom sat on the cold floor. Then a rat scampered into the chamber.

"How d'ye do?" said the rat. "My name is Nibble."

"Tom Truepenny," replied Tom. He was about to shake the rat's hand, and then realised that that would be absurd.

"I'll tell ye a secret," said the rat. "If you give me something to nibble on . . ."

Tom reached into his pocket and found a few crumbs of the scone he had eaten for breakfast that morning.

"That'll do," said the rat. "Aye, that'll do nicely, good sir." *Nibble, nibble, nibble*, went the rat. "Now if you direct your attention to the flagstone which is seventh from the door and third to the left, you might find something beneath it which will tickle your fancy. Well, I must be about my business, looking for something to nibble on. Good day to you, Mr. Tom." With that, the rat scampered off again.

So Tom counted the flagstones, seventh from the door and third to the left, and found that he could put his fingers under this one. He tried to lift it with all his might, but could not budge it more than half an inch. Now he really would need the help of his friends.

Tom set off back down the tunnels, thankful that he had left the acorns to guide him, and climbed up the sixty-six stairs. Gasping for air, he emerged from the knothole, elated to be back in the daylight again. Tom related the course of his travails to his companions, and of the mysterious flagstone, which he had found with the rat's aid. At length they decided that Gabriel should accompany him back through the knothole, while Josiah remained behind to guard the camp against the encroaching nightfall. To this end, they gathered twigs and branches and started a fire. Some of the trellises in the Ruined Garden had fallen, and at Josiah's suggestion they gathered up boards of splintered wood to aid them in lifting the heavy flagstone.

So Tom and Gabriel climbed up the ancient oak and squeezed through the knothole. They descended the spiral stair and threaded their way through the tunnels, easily finding the chamber they sought with the marker acorns to guide them.

Even with both of them lifting, panting and grunting with the effort, they could not raise the flagstone more than an inch. But it was just enough to slip one of the trellis boards under. So with Gabriel lugging at the stone, and Tom inserting board on top of board, inch by inch they managed to heave the thing open. They placed the last board lengthwise as a support. A noxious odor billowed up from the hole.

Without waiting to deliberate who would go down, Tom scrambled down the hole and emerged covered with cobwebs and dust, clutching a mouldering tome under his arm. The support gave way, and the massive flagstone came crashing down. Not pausing to admire their treasure, Gabriel and Tom hastened back to the spiral stair.

At the three-way juncture, they encountered a hideous wraith with leering red eyes glaring out of skeletal sockets. Before they could utter a word, the wraith tried to snatch the book away from Tom, shrieking: "How many centuries have I waited! At last it is mine!" Gabriel quickly drew his sword and with a single stroke dispatched the awful spectre, who collapsed into a pile of bones and turned to dust.

Not dallying to find out if the wraith had companions, they continued on their way to the spiral stair, collecting acorns as they went, so none could follow them. As they surmounted the marble steps, they heard a frantic shrieking from deep in the tunnels and emerged from the knothole shivering with dread. They huddled near the blazing fire until the blush of life returned to their pallid faces.

By the flickering light of the fire, Josiah eagerly began to read the tome they presented him. The pages were yellow and brittle, but the text was still legible:

THE BOOK OF EDEN

A bloated, bloody moon rose over the black mountains to the east. A bone-chilling wind blew from the north, and a lone wolf howled in the unholy wood the west. And all was disconcertingly quiet in the green valley from which they journeyed in the south, as Josiah pored over the eldritch tome—

I AM THE KING

My agony is Infinite. My Ecstasy greater still. I have travelled to the End of Space. I have suffered to the End of Time. I have learnt All That is Known. I have learnt Nothing at All. My followers are legion. I went to the Cross Roads and corrupted a million souls. I told them Together we would storm the Gates of Heaven. I was a Liar. But I had a Secret Charm which made me Irresistible . . .

I wooed a Princess. She was Pure. As Beauty is Truth. As Truth is Beauty. She sat on a Golden Throne. She bathed in a Crystal Pool with iridescent-winged sprites to swathe her in samite. She was Perfection . . .

I seduced her. I tarnished what cannot be tarnished. I fell upon her like a plague of locusts, and ravished her ripe succulent fruit until only a worm-feasted, fly-ravaged core remained. I cradled her skeletal remains in my arms like a babe and lustily sniffed the bouquet of her dying breath like the last rose of summer, inhaling her fragrant soul into my Insatiable Maw . . .

I am the Ultimate Evil.

Josiah shuddered, chilled as deeply as Gabriel and Tom had been when they had braved the underground tunnels. His first impulse was to cast the abominable book into the fire; but it had been such a hard-won treasure, and it would delight their father to add it to his library. So he stowed it in his saddle-bag and curled up by his brothers—one old and one new—and drifted into a deep sleep. But his sleep was disturbed by frightful dreams, for he had opened *The Book of Eden*.

Josiah found himself in a mindless waste outside of time, beyond all space. A Dusty Road traversed the waste wherein it crossed the Dead Road. Here was the Cross Roads. At the Cross Roads were a multitude of creatures—Lurkers and Slithers, Chilluns and Creepers. And there was the Black Shepherd, his face cowled by a hood. He held a crook in his hand.

Josiah followed the Black Shepherd down Dead Road until they came to a house, deep in Dark End Wood. On the gate slept a monstrous Owl, who did not stir as her master past. The house was dead as a doornail, its family tree extinct. The fence was rusty, the windows were cracked, the garden all overgrown with weeds. The Black Shepherd produced a silver key and opened wide the door.

> "*Come inside why don't you?*
> *Come inside with me.*
> *Come inside, yes please do,*
> *Come and have some tea . . .*"

Josiah awoke in a cold sweat. It was just after dawn, and the cock had missed his cue. It was only a dream, or so he thought, but Josiah resolved never again to open that accursed book.

They made an early start, prompted by the indefatigable dragonfly, who buzzed about their heads until Tom, Josiah, and, after much persuasion, the lumbering Gabriel were awake and had donned their linens and gear. Dragonfly showed them a hole in the crumbling wall about the Ruined Garden, and they walked next to their horses down Daisy Path, treading lightly on the forget-me-nots. The morning air was heavy with the scent of lavender, lilac, honeysuckle, and baby's breath, which set Gabriel and Tom in good spirits. Josiah, however, nursed a secret sorrow he dared not tell.

IV. THE DREAM EMERALD

By midday, they arrived at Hexham Town, where the River Tay met her truelove the Tamar and their union was consummated in the Deep Blue Sea. They mounted their horses and followed the dragonfly up Sandy Road until it crossed with Windy Way. Here was Coffin Inn. They housed their horses in the stable and stepped into the tavern for a draught of local ale. A great fire burned in the hearth to drive away the chill, and cheerful voices were raised in song to drown out the sound of the whistling wind. A motley crew of sailors were perched at the bar, clutching their glasses like rigging.

Josiah wandered upstairs, where he met the mistress of the Inn, the widow of Captain Coffin, Goody Sarah. She sat him down to tea up on the widow's walk, then took him down the spiral stair to the library under the cellar.

Here Goody Sarah grew her mushrooms, the mushrooms from which she brewed her tea which was now beginning to take effect. Josiah realized the teacup was slipping from his fingers and shattering on the stone floor, fracturing spirally into infinite shards flying outwards.

Josiah sat under the umbrella of a six-foot-tall blue-spotted mushroom and contemplated the masonry at the base of the wall. Goody Sarah smiled and passed him a long-stemmed bamboo pipe, and the cellar blurred and melted into a garden. Bullfrogs croaked in the pond. Guinea hens squawked in the bushes. One of them poked her head out.

"Gobble-gobble-gobble," she said.

"And good-day to you," replied Josiah courteously.

"Gobble-gobble-gobble," said the guinea hen. "Show me the Emerald. Show me the Emerald."

"Nay, Miss Guinea Hen," said Josiah. "For even if I could show you, which I cannot, I do not know the magic word to open the cedar box."

"Gobble-gobble-gobble," said the guinea hen. "That's easy. That's easy. It's AMEN. It's AMEN . . ."

Just then there was a rustling in the bushes and out stepped a striped raccoon with glowing green eyes staring out hypnotically from behind black rings.

"Allow me to introduce myself," said the raccoon. "My name is Pennyroyal. But you can call me Penny. Everyone else does." Then without another word she slipped into the willow tree, which drooped sadly over the pond.

Enchanted by those green eyes, Josiah followed her into the tree despite the protesting gobble-gobble-gobbles of the guinea hen. The hole looked small at first glance, but when he tried to squeeze into it Josiah found that it widened, accommodating itself to his girth. With a bit of flailing and wriggling he passed through the hole and plopped into a warm dank cloister inside the tree.

Here was a spiral stair of wooden steps all slippery with mould and moss which he began to climb until the wooden steps gave way to dusty stone ones which echoed beneath his boots. At the top of the stair was a mahogany door with a tarnished brass knob, cold to the touch. The door was unlocked and opened, to Josiah's bewilderment, onto a room of the Coffin Inn where Gabriel and Tom were awaiting him. There was no sign of Pennyroyal.

Gabriel had procured passage on a ship from Captain Hawkins, a kinsman of the Drakes. They sailed for the Western Lands on the morrow. So they slept and dreamed sweet dreams. All except Josiah. And in the morning, the dragonfly was gone.

* * *

They set sail on Monday; the dawn was clear and brisk. The good ship *Adelaide* weighed anchor and unfurled her wispy sails, which swelled in the stalwart East Wind. She rode tall across the crested waves, proud like a lady. Gabriel stood at the prow, together with Tom, who stayed with the Drakes, though he had been smitten with love for Katherine, the youngest of the Coffin daughters. He vowed he would return to her one day, and she still lights a candle in her window for him at night, gazing wistfully across the Deep Blue Sea.

Nine ravens had come to roost on all the masts along with an old King Raven, who perched upon the highest mast, his outstretched black wings overshadowing the banner. They answered the cacophonous squawking of the gulls with a regal silence. It spoke of bad tidings. Seasick and fearful, Josiah cloistered himself in his cabin to read from *The Book of Norn:*

> *Only at the witching hour*
> *Will a Raven ever speak,*
> *When blooming like a daemon flower*
> *He opens up his pointed beak.*

So that night, while his brother slept, Josiah crept up the mainmast to the crow's nest to speak with the King Raven.

"O Most Noble Raven," he beseeched the bird. "Tell me what fate you and your worthy company betide. Tell me, who calls upon you at the witching hour."

The raven opened up a single staring eye and fixed it on Josiah. "Who dares call upon Hugin, who sits on the shoulder of the Most Grimm?"

"It is Josiah Drake, the son of Jackson."

"Under whose banner do you sail?"

"Why, the Queen's, of course."

"You lie. You sail for the Shepherd, and I am his banner. I herald the doom which will befall you if you dishonour your word to him. Keep watch and be silent, for he who betrays the words of a raven breaks the ancient trust, and if the trust be broken, a curse will be upon the Drakes which can never be broken. Go, Josiah Drake, the son of Jackson, and call upon me no more."

The raven closed his eye, and Josiah scampered back down the mast. He crawled into bed and wished he could unknow what he knew. The ship rocked and creaked like a cradle, but Josiah did not sleep.

Tuesday's warning: red skies in the morning, and a chill wind blowing down from the North. Still Captain Hawkins steered a true course. Wednesday, storm clouds gathered. Thursday, they threatened, and Friday, they broke. Saturday tossed the *Adelaide* roughly; the waters frothed and churned. The sailors started to pray, each to whatever god watched over him.

Sunday the storm abated. The sky was clear, the water still. The sails hung limp, for there was not the slightest whisper of a breeze. A strange mist began to swirl around the ship.

"'Tis the Ravens which bring us bad luck," cried Gabriel. "I will dispatch their king and be rid is of them."

Josiah in fear grasped Gabriel by the arm.

"What, brother," said Gabriel, anger flashing in his eyes. "Would you stop me?"

Josiah wavered, then unhanded him. "Nay."

Gabriel slung his sword over his shoulder and hoisted himself up the mainmast to face the King Raven.

"Come, Sir Raven," he challenged. "Will you and your brethren be off our ship, or must I dispatch you?"

The King Raven remained silent.

"So be it." Gabriel unsheathed his sword and one of the ravens flew at him, tearing at his skin with sharp talons and pecking at his eyes with its pointed beak. He swung his sword through the air, but only grazed its tail-feathers, too quick was the raven. Then from below, Tom flung a stone with his sling and struck the bird square in the head. The raven fell to the deck, quite dead. The king raven opened up both his eyes, which glared red with rage, and, spreading his majestic black wings, departed the good ship *Adelaide*, together with his company, soaring away west and out of sight.

Gabriel sheathed his sword and joined his fellows on deck. He held up the vanquished bird in triumph.

"Tonight we shall feast on raven's meat!"

The sailors hurrahed. A bonfire blazed on deck that night, and the crew made merry.

> *"Sixteen men on a dead man's chest;*
> *Yo ho ho, and a bottle of rum . . ."*

Josiah, however, sat alone in the crow's nest and read very different verses out of *The Book of Norn*:

Judgment falls on who slays a raven,
But safe is him who stays a craven.

At the witching hour on that moonless night, as the drunken sailors slept, a leviathan arose from the murky depths and wrapped the *Adelaide* in its loathsome embrace. Gabriel awoke too late and reached for the Berserker Potion his father had given him, but found it snatched from his hand by a creeping tentacle. Tom took a stab at the tentacle with a boathook, but to no avail; it slipped back down under the waves, leaving a trail of green ooze behind it.

Alas, the good ship *Adelaide* was sunk without a trace, straight down to Davy Jones's locker, all hands lost—all but one, who floated away quietly on a cedar box—

"And I go
Down below."

* * *

The Hidden God

Josiah Drake, the craven son,
    The son of Jackson Drake,
Was cast adrift and tempest-tost;
    All hope did he forsake.

Josiah Drake was kept afloat
    Upon a cedar ark;
Within the ark a treasure lay,
    An Em'rald in the dark.

At last, half-dead, Drake washed ashore
    Where dwelt the Hidden God.

A sapphire isle, a gloomy place,
    It was the Land of Nod.

Josiah Drake sat on the sand,
    And gazed across the deep;
His brother's death a noble stand,
    And yet it made him weep.

His skin was burnt, his coat in rags,
    And lost his book and sword,
He fell asleep upon the sand,
    And to the House was lured.

Ajar the door into the House,
    He found inside quite small.
And in the House, cat toyed with mouse
    Inside the bedroom wall.

A Herald woke Drake in the night;
    His horse was black as sin.
Josiah thought of taking flight,
    A race he could not win.

The Herald bore a coat of arms,
    Emblazed a yellow sign,
And from his hip he drew a flask,
    Engraved that cruel design.

The Herald dropped the flask athwart
    The toe of Drake's worn boot,

And asked him if he served the Court,
    A question rendered moot.

Josiah could not answer him.
    'Well, from the flask then drink,'
The Herald said to Drake.
    'And tell me what you think.'

The Herald's horse then bore him off,
    And with Drake left the flask.
This hidden drink that he must quaff,
    What was it might he ask.

He pressed the flask to thirsty lips,
    Inside was nectar brown;
And turning bottom's end to up,
    He poured the nectar down.

He nodding dreamt a theatre stage
    Of dancing bones on strings.
The threads were spun in twists of fate
    That spiders know what brings.

One puppet's dance did catch his eye,
    The winged cloaked shape of Death,
Who tightly held a flask in hand
    To catch a man's last breath.

Josiah woke to breaking dawn,
    A spectre now the play.

His hurt was gone; his skin was wan;
    He shrunk now from the day.

The Land of Nod is stark terrain,
    Where winds forever mourn.
The endless rain pours down in vain
    Upon a land forlorn.

The son of Drake kept to the path
    That spiralled up the mount.
A garden met him at its end,
    And empty was the fount.

Atop the gate there perched an owl,
    Whose feathers all were black,
Upon his face a fearsome scowl,
    His claws bared to attack.

The Herald rode up on his horse,
    And stood beside the gate
To usher Drake, and what is worse,
    To seal Josiah's fate.

The trees were bare, no flowers grew,
    No honey in the comb.
The sky was black where once was blue,
    Æthereal the dome.

Within the yard a weeping girl,
    Stone-frozen there for years:

And at her feet there lay a flask;
    The flask was full of tears.

He took the flask in sympathy,
    To sleep his only goal;
He drank it dry to ease the pain,
    And so he lost his soul.

To nodding eyes the roses bloomed,
    Their petals starkest white.
Beneath an opalescent moon,
    Josiah spent the night.

He dreamt about the hidden House,
    Whose Mistress's name was Grey.
She had him to her room for tea
    So like an ass he'd bray.

The dawn came up; no rooster crowed;
    The mist clung to the moat.
Across the moat a ferry rowed,
    The Oarsman like a goat.

The Oarsman then held out his hand:
    'What have you for my fee?'
And hoisting up his worthy pole:
    'That Em'rald would suit me.'

The Herald blocked the Ferryman,
    And paid him with a groat.

'Our guest pays court to Mistress Grey;
    Now row us in your boat.'

Into the gate, his honour foiled,
    Drake saw no other choice.
Around his throat a serpent coiled,
    Until he lost his voice.

He shed his rags and donned a coat,
    A coat of pitchest black.
A silver sword went in his sheath;
    Drake joined the court, alack!

The Queen was grim, her name was Grey,
    A needle in her hand;
She woke by night and slept by day,
    A-counting grains of sand.

The needle pricked Drake's starving vein,
    And drew a drop of blood;
The price was such a tiny pain
    For such a blissful flood.

In dreams the modest House appeared
    A castle bleak and tall.
Shipwrecked upon the Land of Nod,
    Drake sheltered in its wall.

The nectar flowed in streams of gold;
    He craved it like a bee.

It numbed his soul against the cold;
    He loved it as did she.

One day he would climb up the stair
    To meet the Hidden God;
It chilled the spine and prickled skin
    To see the King of Nod.

Upon an oaken throne in chains,
    He found his forebear Jack:
'By turning wheel and grinding stone,
    I bid thee welcome back.'

He bent his knee to Hidden God,
    And mourned the fate of Drakes;
A wolf-wind howled through barren Nod,
    A dreary sound it makes.

Josiah took his place at tea,
    The Queen sat by his side;
They pricked their veins each one of three,
    A kindred kept inside.

The hearth ablaze with dreams of fire,
    They wished their cups with tea:
To each of them his heart's desire,
    Whatever it might be.

Up in his room the Hidden God
    Was kicking up a din;

He would not stop till all was Nod,
    And ev'ry man his kin.

'I am Y^e Olde, Y^e Shepherd Black,
    Now give me what is due;
Thy father paid and so did Jack,
    And now Josiah, you.'

The Em'rald lay inside a box,
    Held fast there by a spell.
There is a word that it unlocks;
    To you the word I'll tell:

'Four feathers lost old Mother Goose;
    One feather made a pen.
The pen with ink four letters wrote;
    The word it spelled: AMEN.'

And now the ark yawned open wide:
    The Em'rald he beheld.
Its beauty was beyond my pen
    That in his hand he held.

Drake slowly crept up stair by stair;
    Like needles on his skin,
The cold did bristle up his hair;
    The walls were closing in.

Atop the stair an oaken door,
    An acorn for a knob.

He turned the knob; it opened wide;
    He heard a stifled sob.

He put a foot across the jamb,
    Wood creaking like a ship;
The Shepherd warned the bleating lamb,
    Lest on the blood he slip.

The attic room was cloaked in dark;
    A candle shed a light.
A jingling sound he then did hark:
    The Hidden God in sight.

Bound up in chains, in chains of lead,
    Hung from a hook, his cage,
While from his arm a river bled,
    The Hidden God did rage.

Upon his brow a golden crown,
    The Em'rald it adorned.
The House began a-falling down;
    The brazen Herald horned.

A full moon hung, ballooned with blood;
    The mountain tumbled down.
Across the island washed a flood,
    And threatened Drake to drown.

Josiah Drake stood on the roof
    To beg the starry sky,

And in the midst of raging storm,
    A Raven heard his cry.

The Raven's claws clasped to his waist,
    And heavenward he flew.
Of angel's warmth he had a taste;
    The devil had his due.

The son came home, his father dead,
    A scapegoat to a god:
A golden crown around his head,
    He was the King of Nod.

* * *

unfinished business

Ezekiel Pitt was an honest Joe, and though but a simple woodsman his manners were never lacking. One day as he was a-wandering home through the dark wood he spot a poor sparrow a-weeping up in the branch of an old yew tree. And goodly Zeke asked, "O Sparrow, why do you weep on such a happy day?"

To which the sparrow replied, "Good sir, my mistress lies sleeping, a-sleeping in the thorn. Till she wakes we will all be ever so forlorn." This news touched Ezekiel's kindly heart and he asked, "Where be this sleepin' miss a-lyin'?"

To which the sparrow replied, "Behind this tree is a path; the path leads onto the House. Behind the house is a garden, behind the garden, a reed. In the midst of the reed is a tangled patch of briar and there sleeps my mistress, a-nestled in the thorn. But take care, good sir, beware the sharp-pointed thorn."

Slinging his axe over his shoulder, Ezekiel started down the long winding path behind the yew tree and soon found himself swallow up by

IV. The Dream Emerald

the thorn. Brambles clung to his ankles and prickly bush rent his britches. The sun began to set and the gnarled and ancient trees cast long wizened shadows across the unhallowed ground. Icy fingers wormed their way under his skin and danced an Irish jig on his bones. The thorn grew thicker, tearing his already tattered coat until he could go no further; the thorn was all around and cold and Ezekiel's thoughts turned to hearth and home. He knelt down to pray.

A golden light shone through an ash tree, a beacon in the darkness, a lantern showing him the way to the Promised Land. With the strength of a hundred men Ezekiel swung his mighty axe and started whacking away at the thorn—*whack–whack–whack*. He was up all night whacking that thorn and come sunup he had cleared away a nice bit of new ground right up to the front door of the house.

But the house is all overgrown with thorn too and there were ten ravens perched upon the roof—nine ravens on the nine gables and the tenth way up on the garret. The tenth raven was a big old bird, the Granddaddy of All Ravens. He knocked on the door and one of the Ravens opened up his eyes. But there was no answer. He knocked again, louder this time, and then he knocked a third time. But the house was locked up tight as a drum.

"Well, that's a fine how'd'yedo," he remarked. And then, all tuckered out from whacking at the thorn all night, he slipped around back to the stable for a snooze. The stable door was open (the horse had already got out) and Ezekiel fell fast asleep on the soft hay.

Ezekiel dreamt of a parlour and in the parlour was a table. Tea was set for five at the table, but only a sad old woman wearing black lace sat there. She silently beckoned him to sit at one of the places, but no one sat at the head of the table. He heard footsteps coming down the stairs—*clip–clop–clip–clop*—then he awoke back in the stable again. It was night. A candle was guttering up in the garret window and languorous shadows moved, so he tried the door again—*knock–knock*—but still no answer came.

"Not exactly Southern hospitality," he muttered to himself.

"Hardly," uttered a voice.

"Who said that?" gasped Ezekiel.

"I did," quoth the Granddaddy Raven who opened up both his eyes.

"Evenin'," returned Ezekiel evenly. "My name's Zeke."

"Mine is Memory. I have been expecting you. At last the deal shall be done and I may fly back to the left shoulder of Old Greybeard, who must be worried that I am lost forever. Now follow the dragonfly. She knows the way."

A sprightly little dragonfly buzzed around Ezekiel's head a couple of times, then flew away and he took off after her in hot pursuit. They tore across the garden of graves until they came to the pond. At the pond was the stone, and at the stone they rested looking at the reflection of the silvery moon shimmering on the waters. Then dragonfly led Ezekiel into the Yellow'd Reed, and waiting at the middle of the Yellow'd Reed was the Rampant Hare. Here was the briar path, the tangled thick of thorn where golden-curled Mary lay sleeping. A hummingbird flew down and turned into a little pixy with cowslips in her hair and wearing a green gown. She motioned to the Rampant Hare.

"Tea for two, I think." The Rampant Hare bowed down low and dutifully complied. Ezekiel solemnly took one of the cups and began to carry it through the briar.

"Careful now," ordered Sabrina. "Step where I tell you. Step to the left, now to the right—gently now, over the root—there. What a pretty white rose she is."

Ezekiel pressed the cup of elderflower tea to her lips, and that is how the man all tattered and torn kissed the maiden all forlorn. Come sunup the ravens had left Old Ettinfell.

> *Miss Mary Drake and Pitt were wed*
> *And joined together in one bed.*
> *And betwixt these lovers mild*
> *Bore they forth a Shepherd child.*

IV. THE DREAM EMERALD

"Pa picked up a strop of rawhide leather
and began to beat his wayward child..."

– V –
THE BROKEN PROMISE

Joe Pitt grew up on his daddy's farm. There were chickens in the coop, apples in the tree, corn in the field and snakes in the grass. His house had a chimbley and a weathervane on top. Joe was the oldest of seven children; the other six were girls. Their names were Mary, Annie, Mollie, Lizzie, Hester, and Sykes.

Joe had his hands full milking cows in the morning, tossing hay with a pitchfork at noon, and picking corn all day long. But when the evening came and the sun was going down behind the old oak tree, he liked nothing more than to sit on the bank of the River Tay and listen to the waters go rushing by.

Across the river there was a willow tree, limbs outstretched wide as if to beckon him to embrace her swollen bosom. He would stare long at her graceful curves as she slowly swayed back and in the gentle summer breeze. But the river came between them.

Ofttimes, especially towards the dog-days of August, he would stay out late at night missing his supper to go down by the rushing river and watch his beloved tree dancing her restless dance by the light of the silvery moon. Joe would come home to find his family all gone to bed and a plateful of vittles left out by a worrisome mother.

It was not until his chores started suffering that Pa took notice of the errant boy. Joe had failed to rise early enough to milk the cows, and he had been slipping away from picking corn in the field to steal a few minutes down by the river with his tree. Until one morning as he was set in his accustomed roost on the bank, he was paid a visit by his sister Sykes. Her neck was arched and graceful.

"So here you are, Joe," she said. "Whatever do you do night after night down here by the river?"

"I jest set here," he replied. "Set here and watch yon tree. Ain't she purdy?"

"Joe," began Sykes gravely, "you best come home for supper tonight."

"And if I don't?"

"Then Pa'll prob'ly come down here an' drag you back by the scruff of the neck to give you a tannin'. He's in a right fury, he is, on account of you been missin' chores an' such." Joe had fearful memories of being punished by his father in the past, so he resignedly abandoned his nightly vigil and followed Sykes up the trail home.

Dinner was already set and the family seated at table, Pa and Ma at each end and the children along both sides. Sykes took her place and one chair remained vacant as it must have been for many an evening meal.

"Come and be seated for grace," Pa ordered. Joe meekly acquiesced. The Pitts bowed their heads in prayer.

"For that which we are about to receive, may the Lord make us truly grateful. Amen." It was suppertime.

The dishes were passed around in silence but for the clatter of silver spoons against china. Roast beef, potatoes, cornbread, cabbage. Each member of the family waited patiently for the others to be served before settling in to eat, which they did with the diligence of farm animals. At last Pa spoke.

"Joe, what cause have you for missing your chores?"

A pause ensued. "I been a-setting down by the river."

"Setting down by the river ain't no excuse for missing your chores. You have been guilty of sloth, boy. I forbid you to set by the river any more. I want you to set down to supper with the rest of your family; I want you up in the morning early to milk the cows. And I want you to be diligent about picking corn during the day because you are my only son. I won't say another word on the matter." And he did not. But Joe did not forget the words he had already said. They echoed in his head that evening as his ma rocked in her chair stitching that same old stitch, back and forth. They echoed in his head as he lay awake in bed that night long after any decent Christian should be asleep. And they echoed in his head as he crept out his bedroom window and scampered down down the angled roof-beams under the jagged crescent moon gashing the evil sky like a reaper's scythe.

His tree was waiting for him, a burning star wreathed in her tangled bough. Joe feverishly watched her dance, faster and faster, spurred on by a sudden gust of wind. "Dance, tree. Dance!" Then he felt a hand on his right shoulder. Joe's blissful reverie was abruptly shattered by the sight of his father's grim face, cold and chiselled as stone, eyes belying not a hint of feeling.

Meekly Joe followed his pa up the trail, like a lamb to the slaughter, into the stable where Pa picked up a strop of rawhide leather and began to beat his wayward child slowly, methodically, forty times. The deed was done without a word from Pa and without a cry from Joe, who afterwards lay whimpering on the soft blood-soaked hay. Then Pa took up the Pitt Family Bible, an ancient and cherished tome, gleaming black and leather.

"I seen the way you was looking at that tree," Pa said in the solemnest of tones. "I seen and I fear for your soul. There's devil's work in it. I want you to put your right hand on the Family Bible and swear you won't be looking at that tree any more. Do you swear it?"

"I swear it," sobbed Joe.

"In the name of Our Lord and Master Jesus Christ?"

"In the name of Our Lord and Master Jesus Christ."

"Now git to bed, boy. Git!" And Joe ran like a rabbit, ran past his worrisome mother who stood at the stable door ready to smother him in her arms, ran up the stairs until he lay shivering in his bed again, shivering in spite of the sweltering summer heat. He pulled his blankets up over his head to blot out the leering crescent moon in the sky like a half-shut eye. And still Joe did not sleep. And still Joe did not sleep.

The next morning Joe rose early to milk the cows. He tossed hay with pitchfork and diligently picked corn in the field under the blazing August sun. His sister Sykes brought him a dipperful of water in the afternoon, which he drank down without a word and then returned to his picking. Suppertime came, table was set, grace was said, and vittles were eaten under the solemn gaze of Pa Pitt without a word about the night before. Fireplace burned, stitches were sewn, rocking-chair rocked, and then all the children were packed off to bed: Sykes, Hester, Lizzie, Mollie, Annie, Mary. And Joe. He kissed his mother and went to bed. But Joe did not sleep.

He waited for his sisters to sleep. He waited for Ma to sleep. He waited for Pa to sleep. Especially Pa. He waited for the midnight hour, for the churchbell to chime one. Two. Three. Then he took a gunnysack out from under his bed and slung it over his shoulder. Joe crept out the window and scurried across the angled roof-beams with the stealth of a cat.

A wolf-wind was howling, churning the waters of the river to froth. A slender sickle-moon, sharper even than her sister of the night before, hung low in the sky, dangling over the top of the tree like a silver crown. A black owl was perched in the highest branch, staring at him with fierce predatory eyes. Joe plunged into the River Tay and struggled to stay afloat in the raging, ravenous waters, thrashing against the yawning, cold currents which threatened to hurtle him into oblivion. But nothing could stay Joe from his course. The tree danced. Still the tree danced.

There was a hole in the tree, not big enough for a full-grown man, but big enough for Joe, who crawled into it, an innocent babe in the woods, sliding through velvet moss which soothed his tortured skin, burnt by the sun and lashed by leather. The tree rocked him back and forth. And Joe slept.

In his dreams Joe was by a pond. On the pond swam a graceful swan, with noble neck, white-feathered; the swan swam on the golden sun-dappled pond. In the arched back of the noble swan were forty red gashes, a wounded white swan was she. She trailed blood in the water.

When Joe awoke he found himself at the foot of the tree all covered with some kind of honey. He washed himself in the cold waters of the Tay and headed north. As he hugged the flowing curves of the river, he thought he heard singing. Joe followed the song and swung onto a trail off the river which swooped gracefully into the valley down below, a valley dotted with daisies, the valley of shadows. A gloomy place was the valley of shadows, with craggy rock walls where serpents make their nests, how unlike the sun-dappled green meadows on the other side of the river.

At the end of the valley was a many-angled house. In the back of the house lay Dark End Wood, like a great sprawling garden. Mr. Wright lived in that house with his wife. His wife's name was Penny. They were good to Joe when they saw him coming all tattered and torn and wet from the river. They invited him in for tea.

Mrs. Wright set a nice tea with great big cups and silver spoons and even some china-oranges which she pulled out of the cupboard. They didn't ask him where he came from. They didn't ask him where he was going. They didn't ask him to stay. Penny had a long neck and took a shine to Joe. Joe had nowhere else to go.

The Wrights drank a lot of tea. They drank it morning, noon, and night. Days passed in swirling cups. Penny found gooseberry pies in the cupboard. Joe had nowhere else to go.

The Wrights had a lot of teacups. They were all were white. And all the spoons were silver. Still Joe had nowhere else to go.

Then Penny asked Joe if he would like to take a walk in the wood. Joe said that he would. It was nightfall when they stepped through the door into the mouth of the wood. Branches leered, a black owl hooted, and Joe turned around and found that Penny was gone. Just her ghost weeping in the shadows.

In a fork of willow roots a girl had fallen, her white neck gracefully arched and there were gashes in her back. A shift of feathers lay beside her. Joe stowed the shift in his gunnysack, and wrapped the girl in his tattered coat. He led her by a star through a garden of gravestones shining in the moon like the petals of a white rose until they came to a house with nine gables. The front door was open as if it were his and Joe lived in that house with his girl Jenny. He hid the shift in a box in the attic.

They stayed in that house for forty days and, maybe, forty nights. They drank the tea he made from the honey that trickled out of the yew which grew by the house. No gooseberry pies were found in the cupboard, no china-oranges, not even a bone. And every night the attic would creak. Creak went the attic. *Crrreeak!*

V. THE BROKEN PROMISE

At Christmastime a stranger came. He bore a staff like a shepherd. The stranger knocked it on the door. *Rat-tat-tat. Rat-tat-tattick.* Joe invited him in and offered him tea; this the stranger spurned. The stranger spoke of the Deep Blue Sea and said he would return.

The stranger called a second time. This time he brought a book. He still declined to drink the tea. He left the book upon the table and told Joe, "Take a look."

That night Joe climbed up to the attic, surmounting crooked stair. Open door. Open book. Open box, be ware!

Joe scaled the ladder to the garret, higher than the gables. From his lofty perch he saw all the Dark End Wood. He saw Mr. Wright's house, he saw the valley of shadows. At the end of the earth the River Tay coiled like an adder. With a flurry of feathers falling like petals from a rose the white swan soared away. Grateful to Joe for healing her wounds, Jenny flew back to the golden sun-dappled pond. Joe was all alone in the house, alone with two cups of tea. He would find the pond one day. And a cygnet moon was born, singing.

*

*

*

O ivory neck,
O delicate wings,
What irony-wreck
She elegant brings.
O . . .

Across the wood a river coil'd,
Within it lay a pond;
Beside the pond there stood a house,
A house of dark despond.

Childe Signet was the son of Swann,
    A spindle-Drake was he;
His mother bore him by the pond,
    Before his memory.

His father kept the little boy
    From roaming in the wood;
His father brooded long and hard,
    And much he understood.

There was no bread on Signet's plate,
    No tea to warm his pot;
The poor boy dined on crumbs and crust,
    And hunger was his lot.

Three sisters by the river ran,
    Their dresses purest white,
Named Em & Ruth & Henriette,
    The young 'un like a sprite.

The falling rain washed clean the stones
    Upon the water's edge;
The stones were smooth as velvet moss,
    And hidden in the sedge.

They looked for shelter in the wood,
    And found therein a shack;
They knocked upon the moulding door,
    And opened it a crack.

V. THE BROKEN PROMISE

They found no one inside the house,
    Though wood was freshly cut.
They found a pot a-brim with stew;
    To them it seemed a glut.

The sisters at the table sat;
    The sisters ate the stew;
The sisters lit the twigs of wood,
    And blew upon it—few!

There was a bed for Emily;
    There was a cot for Ruth;
Up in the attic Betty slept;
    She liked it best in truth.

She dreamt about a raftered house
    Where bats hung upside-down;
They craved her lengthy iv'ry neck
    As white as her silk gown.

Next morning there was piping tea
    Upon the tabletop,
With china cup and silver spoon,
    And honey fit to drop.

Before her sisters Betty woke,
    And drank the pixy-tea;
She wandered lost into the wood,
    A little girl was she.

She strayed into a briar patch,
    A prickly snarl of thorn.
It ript apart her pretty dress,
    In tatters it was torn.

She stumbled through the darkened wood,
    A little girl forlorn,
Upon her knees a-weeping soft,
    And then she heard a horn.

A horse's hooves the forest stirred;
    A huntsman Betty found.
She curled up on the velvet moss,
    Which carpeted the ground.

He bore her to the House of Ashe,
    Beyond the river's bend;
A rolling carpet in the hall,
    Its master at the end.

Lord Ashe gave Betty pretty gifts,
    Red ribbons for her hair,
Three turtle doves, a new white dress,
    Which made her witching fair.

Her room was at the house's peak,
    And from it she could see
Yᵉ Darken'd Wood and much beyond;
    She pondered it with tea.

Her hair grew longer by the year;
    She braided it in knots.
The House of Ashe was near the pond,
    And Signet in her thoughts.

Childe Signet Drake had heard the call;
    A horn blew in the wood;
He saddled horse and rode it tall;
    His father understood.

He rode beside the River Tay
    By which a willow grew;
An owl hooted in the day,
    The sound it made: a-HOO!

A river ran, a crooked stream;
    It ran a crooked mile—
A winding trail, a tricksy dream;
    The black owl cracked a smile.

The sloping path gave way to bog;
    His horse stuck fast in mud;
And Drake sunk hip-deep in the mire;
    The black owl wanted blood.

Childe Signet Drake slumped in a slough,
    Above him perched the owl;
And then from far away he heard
    A distant chilling howl.

A rider rode out from the wood,
    His steed as black as pitch;
He dragged the Drake out of the slough,
    Bedevilled by the witch.

The rider led him through the wood,
    A trail of tears and thorn,
Which rent his coat and drew his blood;
    Drake chased the knight till dawn.

This was the house of hope forlorn;
    It was an occult place;
The rider led Drake through the thorn,
    And never showed his face.

Drake mulled his plight with much chagrin,
    And lingered at the door;
A glass of wine await him in:
    Lord Ashe's crimson lure.

Behind the house a garden lay,
    Where roses grew and thorn;
Lost Betty took her refuge there,
    And listened for the horn.

A narrow path wound through the thorn
    Which o'er the valley crept;
Lord Ashe bade Signet venture in,
    For there a dragon slept.

Lord Ashe gave Drake a book and sword,
    A ruby for them due,
For rubies graced the Dragon's hoard,
    And more than just a few.

The pixies danced beneath the moon,
    In dresses that were grass,
'Neath cowslips they were wont to swoon,
    A jack for ev'ry lass.

Childe Signet watched them by a tree;
    The pixies took his hand,
And spunhimspunhimspunhim—whee!
    Till on his back he land.

The Pixy-Queen stood on a hill;
    Her skin was white as snow.
With raven hair, or blacker still,
    Her name was Lady Jo.

At night would Betty leave the house
    And dance beneath the moon.
She spunanspunanspun till dawn
    Like tea stirred with a spoon.

The pixies drank from blooms like bees,
    From nectar in a bowl,
And in the meadow danced in threes,
    A dance to steal one's soul.

The Queen watched Drake dance with her kin,
    And offered him some wine;
A pretty maid served it to him,
    And herbs on which to dine.

The Queen gave Drake a silver key,
    A lanthorn too she gave,
So in the darkness he could see
    The dragon in the cave.

The cavern's mouth lay in the stone,
    Well hidden by wild gorse,
Which Signet had to brave alone,
    No room to ride his horse.

Childe Signet crept down darkened stair;
    The cold pricked up his skin;
It bristled up his golden hair;
    The walls came closing in.

The Dragon hoarded rubies red
    Down in his putrid cave;
He slept with jewels for a bed,
    To darkness but a slave.

Har! Har!

– VI –
Gooseberry Tea

Betty Jo Spindledrake was deep in the wood when she spotted a golden egg. As she strayed towards it she was snared by a thicket, a twisty thicket of thorn. The thorn tore at her dress, her pretty dress, her dress of purest white. The thorn coiled around her wrists and ankles, tricksy little thorn. The thorn scratched and scraped her delicate skin, that terrible thirsty thorn, so very thirsty for her ruby-red blood. Poor Betty Jo.

"Allow me to introduce myself," interjected a snake. "You s-s-seem in need of s-s-some ass-sis-s-stance."

"Oh, good sir," pleaded Betty. "Please help me out of this terrible thicket of thorn."

"That's-s-s s-s-simple enough," said the snake. "Jus-s-st turn your wris-s-sts-s-s and ankles-s-s widdershins-s-s and you will be free."

Betty did so and to her joy found her limbs easily extricated from the entangling thicket.

"I thank you, dear serpent," she said. "How can I ever repay you?"

"My work is its own reward, child," said the snake modestly. "Though perhaps there is one favour you could bestow on me."

"Anything, gentle serpent."

"Will you make tea for my master tonight?"

"It would be an honour to make tea for your master tonight."

"At the s-s-stroke of midnight then. Come to his hous-s-se at the end of the wood. Don't be late. And don't forget to bring goos-s-seberries-s-s." The snake slithered away leaving behind the ghost of a rattle and a silver key.

Betty was frantic, for she knew not where the gooseberries grew. She ran herself ragged searching the wood. She looked high and low in the valley of the shadows. She combed the banks of the river, but she could find not hide nor hair of a single gooseberry. Betty threw herself at the feet of a willow weeping bitter tears. A fox sidled up beside her and asked, "Wherefore do you weep, little girl?"

"Oh good sir," wept Betty, "I have promised to bring gooseberries for tea tonight, but I know not where the gooseberries grow."

"Alas, nor do I," said the fox. "But I do know of one who does."

"Please tell me," begged Betty. "For I cannot break a promise."

"The owl who perches atop the yew. He can tell you where the gooseberries grow. Or at least give you a clew."

"I thank you, dear fox," said Betty. "How can I ever repay you?"

"It would give a poor fox distinction if you would make tea for my master tonight."

"That is the least I can do for one who is so noble and true."

"Then come to his house which is on the highest hill at the end of the wood." The fox skulked back into the wood.

So Betty went to the yew which grew by the water's edge. The wizened owl who was perched atop the highest branch opened up his all-seeing eye and crooned, "Who goes there, friend or foe? It has been so long since anyone has visited me, I surely could have neither."

"I am but a little girl," she replied. "Stricken by misery and woe."

"What misery is it which could strike woe into the heart of a little girl?"

"I have promised to bring gooseberries for tea tonight, but I know not where they grow."

"That is a grave misfortune indeed," agreed the owl.

"A fox told me that you could tell me where the gooseberries grow."

"Then on a crooked path hath he set you. I cannot tell you where the gooseberries grow. But I can tell you of one who can."

"Oh most wise owl, tell me. Pray tell me who."

"Why, it is as plain as the nose on your face, child. Only a goose would know where the gooseberries grow."

"I thank you, dear owl," said Betty. "How can I ever repay you?"

"The company of such a pretty girl is payment enough," said the owl.

"But if you would be so kind, there's a good girl, kind enough to make tea for my master?"

"It would be a privilege to make tea for the master of such a stately and venerable owl," said Betty.

"His house is on the highest hill beyond the Yellow'd Reed at the end of the wood. Come tonight and don't forget to fetch a basket to carry the gooseberries in." The owl outstretched his black-feathered wings and flew away.

So Betty went on. She staggered down the creek. She sallied into gloomy meadow, wind whistling through winter-bare elms. She treaded the path of creeping thorns—gently lest the sharp-pointed thorns prick her tender bare feet, vines with claws so eager to tear at her flowing skirts. On and on she trod, step by ginger step till at last she came upon the pond; the icy waters quivered in the bloody hue of the setting sun.

A gaggle of geese wearing red and white bonnets waddled by the pond. They clucked at her and sang her a silly song:

> "Gooseberry gooseberry,
>
> Where do you grow?
>
> Where the mud is green,
>
> Where the waters flow;
>
> That, silly goose,
>
> Is where gooseberries grow."

So Betty scampered to the north side of the pond where the waters flowed from the yawning mouth of the river. Here bubbled a pool of emerald-green mud and in the pool of emerald green mud grew the gooseberry bush. A goose waddled thither and sized Betty up in a gander. And the goose said, "Jenny's the name, how do you do miss? If basket's need weavin', I know how to do this.

> "A penny's the charge,
>
> For handles or not;

No matter how large,

As my mother me taught.

"*In a jiffy I'll spin*

Your basket, I will,

For pennies are thin,

And babies are ill."

"Oh goosie," said Betty. "I do need a basket, but I haven't a penny or even a farthing."

"Ah, well," said Betty. "Spinning's its own reward." And in a jiffy she had spun the finest of baskets (with handles no less) out of the reeds that grew by the pond.

"I thank you, miss goosie," said Betty. "I do not have a penny, but would you come with me to tea tonight at my master's house at the end of the wood?"

"It would be an honour for such a humble goose," said Jenny, and together they gathered the gooseberries which grew in the green mud by the mouth of the river.

Word spread like wildfire amongst the gaggle of gossipy geese, and one by one each goose waddled up to Betty to ask if she could come.

"May I come to tea with you at the house on the high hill at the end of the wood?" asked Agatha first for she was the oldest and boldest goose.

"Of course you may, dear goosie," said Betty. "For your cousin has done me a great favour."

"And I?" asked Tillie, who was Agatha's twin. "May I come to tea with you at the house on the highest hill past the yellow'd reed at the end of the dark and treacherous wood?"

"I would be delighted," said Betty graciously, "if you joined your cousin, sister, and me." And so on down the line they asked until the whole gaggle—"And I?"—yes, even little Jo was invited.

The geese got all gussied up in their finest red and white checkered bonnets and wrapped blue ribbons around their necks, which were held up straight with pride. And so with a gaggle of geese in tow and a basket full of gooseberries around her wrist, Betty set off into the yellow'd reed.

They passed many a creepy cottage where mole eyes stared out from behind half-drawn curtains. They watched Betty and her geese stroll by and by; they watched with covetous eyes craving to have Betty for supper. But wanting is not the same as having, and those hungry, hungry eyes watched each goose pass one by one. Then the curtains closed.

The path became steeped and narrow and the geese had to waddle single file up and up the sloping trail winding around the hill like a corkscrew once, snarling thorn clutching at skirts and tail-feathers; twice, snakes slithering in and out of knotty vines, thrice around that mole-hill of a mountain.

At the top of the hill stood a ruined house, gables grown over with moss, vines crawling into broken windows. Betty turned the silver key in the rusty lock and the door creaking open wide. Jenny spun a broom out of a stick of birch and some straw from the stable, and swept the floor clean of dust and glass.

Betty found a pot of clay in the kitchen to make her tea. Agatha fetched water from the well in a tin bucket. Tillie sifted through the ashes in the stove till she found a single glowing ember, and she blew and blew whilst Lucy laid kindling and wood until they coaxed that ember into a spark and that spark into a roaring fire. Prudence found a clean cloth in the linen closet and spread it over the oaken table in the parlour. Irma found bone china cups in the cupboard and Jo silver spoons in the drawer.

Betty brewed her berries in that old clay pot and set it down on a silver tray in the middle of the table. There was a wind at the door and the geese began to sing.

> As was foretold creeps Signet Drake
> Into the Dragon's cave;
> Now open up Y^e Buke of Olde,
> Or naught your soul can save.

His name is BALOR, Child of Wyrme,
    The master of this cave;
In darkest depths he makes his home
    Alive and in a grave.

From plunderers he guards his hoard,
    His nest of rubies red;
His hide protects him from the sword,
    To sleep well in his bed.

A chill crept up Childe Signet's spine;
    He cracked Y^e Olden Buke.
It fell right open to a line;
    He screwed his eyes to look.

There is an herb whose name is stithe,
    Which eats a dragon's skin.
Who daubs it thickly on his sword
    The battle sure will win.

There was a hill deep underground,
    And in this hill a hole;
And in this hole within a hill,
    There lived a toothless mole.

'I'll tell 'ee where the stithe all grows;
    Yes, I know where indeed.
This toothless mole Old Willie knows,
    But you must meet my need.

'A steep price I must ask of thee:
　　Thy bawling first-born son.
　I hope you'll not think less of me;
　　To Willie deal is done.

'The stithe grows wild next to the brook,
　　And with it daub thy sword,
　As so it says in Elder Booke
　　To win Y^e Dragon's hoard.'

So Signet rushed down to the brook,
　　And there he found the stithe;
　He daubed his sword as says Y^e Booke,
　　And then he felt so blithe.

Signet crossed the creaking brook on nine slippery stones. Across the brook was a gloomy grey meadow where nothing grew but thistle. In the midst of the meadow stood a little stone house with a shin-bone for a knocker. A feeble yellow flame flickered in the window. Signet strode up to the front door and gave it three raps. *Rat-tat-tat.* The door opened a crack and an old woman peered out from behind, silhouetted in the dim light.

"Who be ye?" she croaked.

"Good even, madam," said Signet courteously. "I am a lost wayfarer in search of the dragon's lair." The door opened wide and Signet beheld a toothless crone dressed all in black and tatters.

"Come in, sir," she said. "Come and rest yer bones. I'll see what I kin fetch ye." The old widow bade Signet sit in a creaky oak chair and darted to the kitchen. She was surprisingly nimble. She returned with a dry crust of bread on a silver platter which she put on the clothless mahogany table.

"Alas, 'tis last o' larder," she sighed. "Put kettle on though."

She sprang back into the kitchen and returned with a silver teapot and two cracked china cups. The old widow poured a cup of warm water for Signet and one for herself, which she eagerly slurped. Ever the gentleman, Signet took a bite of the empty bread and a sip of the empty tea. There was a wind and a clatter of chains at the door, followed by ten sharp raps. *A-tat-ta-tat-tat. Rat-ta-tat-tattick.*

"That'll be my grandson. Hide in yon chest, fer my grandson be very jealous o' strangers." So quick as a fox, Signet jumped into the chest in the corner of the room and closed the lid whilst the Old Widow hastily cleared the cups. It was the DRAGON.

"Arrr! What have ye fer my sup, Grann?" roared Balor.

GRANN:	Naught but yon crust o' bread.
BALOR:	Har! Har! Nane-the-less I'll feast well to-night.
GRANN:	On what'll ye feast if not yon bread?
BALOR:	On an Englishman come into my lair.
GRANN:	'Ow'll ye ketchum?
BALOR:	Withun a riddle.
GRANN:	What sort o' riddle shell he hev?
BALOR:	His riddle shell be a riddle in three fits.
GRANN:	What will be the first fit?
BALOR:	Tonight when I feast, what will my spoon be?
GRANN:	What will yer spoon be?
BALOR:	The rib ev a whale! That will be my silver spoon.
GRANN:	What will be the second fit?
BALOR:	Tonight when I feast, what will my wine-glass be?
GRANN:	What will yer wine-glass be?
BALOR:	An old horse's hoof. That will be my wine-glass.
GRANN:	An' the third? What'll the third fit be?
BALOR:	Tonight when I feast, what will my roast be?
GRANN:	What will yer roast be?
BALOR:	Tonight I shall feast on an Englishman.

"Har! Har!" The door opened, and with a wind and a whistle the Dragon was gone. Signet crept out of the chest and with a nod to the Old Widow slipt out of the little stone house. The toothless crone rocked in her hunchbacked wicker rocking-chair and cackled quietly to herself.

There was a cavern within the cavern at the far end of the barren meadow, and into the cavern's mouth was Signet swallowed. The trail inside was twisty and narrow; downwards the path sloped coiling under the earth like a corkscrew: once, a flock of bats brushed by his head; twice, adders hissed in knotty nests. Thrice around and he had crossed into the lair of the dragon.

The dragon's lair was stark and spare, strewn with bones everywhere. In the midst of the lair was a heap of bones piled almost to the ceiling. Here was housed the dragon's hoard. Red eyes glittered in the darkness.

"I smell yer English blood," bellowed Balor, sable wings outstretched wide. "Speak the name of him who dares to trespass on my lair."

"Signet Drake, the Son of Swann, at your service."

"Answer me my Riddle-Three, Signet Drake, Son of Swann: tonight when I feast, what will my spoon be?"

"A hard nut to crack," said Signet. "But let me see . . . Could it be—the rib of a whale?"

"Arrr!" roared the dragon. "You are a clever 'un. Answer my the second fit: tonight when I feast, what will my wine glass be?"

"A pretty puzzle," said Signet. "But let me see . . . Could it be—an old horse's hoof?"

"Arrr!" roared the dragon, thrashing the tip of his tail. "Too clever by far. Answer me the third fit: tonight when I feast, what will my roast be?"

"A conundrum to be sure," said Signet. "But let me see . . . Could it be that tonight you feast on English BLOOD!"

The shrieking dragon reared up and tore blindly with his talons, which Signet dodged. Climbing up the dragon's scaly back, Signet plunged his herb-daubed sword into Balor's neck and dispatched the scaly beast into oblivion. A river of black blood flowed across the cavern's floor.

Digging through the pile of bones, the knight found a glittering teardrop red ruby which he put into his pocket. At the far end of the lair was a gate, and behind the gate was a stair. He climbed the stair and at the top was a door. SIR SIGNET turned the silver key in the lock and walked through the door at the stroke of midnight to sit down to tea.

– VII –
Jack the Hunter

Sir John Drake wore a scarlet coat,
    His shots were always crack,
And such a dashing form he cut,
    They called him Hunter Jack.

Now Hunter Jack he had a horn,
    And on it did he blow
Tantivy oh so loud and clear
    The country all did know.

Into the gnarled and twisted thorn
    The cunning fox did run;
The trail was hot and Jack was vexed
    By how low hung the sun.

Then Tom his faithful hound did scent
    A swiftly running hare,
Who ran into the prickly thorn;
    They followed him in there,

Into the land that lies in thorn,
    A-girded by a stream.
A woman washed a veil a-torn,
    And sang a wistful dream.

'O, I was once a bonny lass,
    And now my looks have failed;
I never look into a glass,
    And wear my face a-veiled.'

'Good even, miss,' said Hunter Jack.
    'How far is it to town?
More than a mile? Pray, tell me not.
    (I like your scarlet gown.)'

The woman said, 'I'll tell 'ee this,
    And never do I lie:
Two miles it is, the gospel truth,
    Or as the crow may fly.'

Jack tipped his goose a-feather'd hat,
    And waved to her good-bye;
He rode a mile or maybe two,
    Or as the crow may fly.

Long down the muddy road Jack rode,
    While rain came pouring down;
His scarlet coat was sopping wet
    When he pulled into town.

The town was overgrown with thorn;
    The alleys stank of piss,
And Jack passed by a covered door,
    Whereunder stood a miss.

'How fare you now, my good sir knight?
    It seems to me quite ill.
Perhaps you'd care to spend the night,
    Or else you'll catch a chill.

'I have an oaken table set
    With sweetmeats, fruit, and wine;
I'll berth your horse in stable walls
    If with me you will dine.'

Jack feasted on her warm sweetmeats,
    And drunk deep of her wine;
He drunk until he could no more
    Walk in the straightest line.

'John, you may call me Salomé;
    I've many names beside,
And many men I've lured to me,
    To lay with them bestride.

'Now sit and watch my sacred dance,
    Y^e Dance of Seven Veils,
And may it put you in a trance
    In which my will prevails.'

'But madam, I would never kiss
    A slattern so unclean;
Go to the stream and bathe thyself,
    To other eyes unseen.'

'John, I shall dance with seven veils,
    And kiss thy ruby lips!
And if my face's charm me fails,
    I'll tempt thee with my hips.'

The vixen dropped her outer veil,
    With silver was it sewn;
But Jack held fast and on his horn
    Tantivy loud was blown.

And then another veil came down,
    Pure ebony it was;
She was the fox who in the thorn
    Held Jack's cock in her jaws.

The third veil came a-tumbling down;
    It was a veil of blood.
Jack's purebred in its stable woke
    Up to a crimson flood.

The fourth veil fell, of emerald;
    The fifth was ruby-red;
The sixth veil was of diamond,
    And now the night had fled.

A ray of sun through darkness peeked,
    For it was time for dawn;
Jack lifted up Y^e Golden Veil
    And banished then the thorn.

This was the cock that crowed the dawn,
    Jack's stolen Chanticleer;
The vixen with the shadows fled,
    With nothing else to fear.

Jack rode back to Old Ettinfell;
    He'd dodged his blackest fate—
His cock in hand, a tale to tell,
    And Pertelot await.

"O golden hair, O golden hair,
I sang for thee, O golden hair."

– VIII –
Fiddler Jack

Jack Drake, the son of Hunter John,
    Was not a hunter's son;
To something else was his heart drawn,
    And all else did he shun.

Jack found a fiddle in the walls—
    A vile rat showed him where—
With catgut for its purring strings,
    A bow of horse's hair.

There was a daisy-dotted place
    Where Jack would play unseen,
And to his father's great disgrace
    They called it Fiddler's Green.

So gently would Jack coax his strings
    That even birds would hark,
And pixies streamed from underground
    When daylight ebbed to dark.

The pixies danced beneath the trees;
    They danced in twos and threes;
They spunanspunanspunan—whee!—
    Like petals in the breeze.

A pixy-maid caught Jack's shy gaze,
    And Myrrha she was called;
With cowslips in her golden hair,
    The fiddler was enthralled.

'O golden hair, in verdant gown,
    So beauteous to see,
O golden hair will you let down
    Your golden hair for me?'

The fiddler's father feared for Jack,
    That he should have a trade;
And many times he called his son,
    And many times he say'd:

'My boy, thy fiddle thou must quit,
    If e'er thou mean'st to thrive.'
But Jack just tossed his tangled hair:
    'Nay, not while I'm alive!

'If I my bow should cease to raise,
    They'd think that I've gone mad!
For many are the joyous days
    With music I have had.'

And Jack returned to Fiddler's Green
    To play his witchy tune,
And pixies danced for him unseen
    Beneath the milk-white moon.

'O I won't be my father's Jack,
    And Myrrha is my Jill,
For she will be the fiddler's wife,
    With music when she will.'

The slithy snake was jealous of
    Fair Myrrha's love for Jack;
He bit her on her iv'ry heel—
    I rue the day, alack!

Salt sorrow flow'd from Jack's blue eyes;
    He cradled Myrrha's husk.
The mourning dove soft cooed a dirge
    As night replaced the dusk.

'O woe O woe,' wailed Fiddler Jack.
    'My truelove now is gone.
My truelove now is far below,
    But ashes now, and bone.'

A cat stepped out from someplace dark,
    Her fur was sleek and grey.
'I'll take you to the Land of Nod
    To try the King to sway.

'If you can lull him with your song,
    Your love he may return.
To you her soul does most belong;
    For you her heart does yearn.'

Rejoicing at the grey cat's news,
    Jack followed her in haste;
He journeyed to the Land of Nod,
    A gloomy rainy waste.

There only thorn and thistle grew,
    And mournful winds did moan.
Jack trod upon a tricksome path,
    A catwalk of wet stone.

A slack-jawed dog crouched at the gate,
    A snarling hungry ward.
The grey cat's fur stood on its end;
    Jack struck a soothing chord.

The dog left off its ugly growl,
    And yipped his love for Jack.
Jack tickled him beneath the jowl,
    And didn't once look back.

The castle of the King was stark,
    And open was the door,
No tapestries upon the walls,
    No carpets on the floor.

The King sat on an onyx throne,
    His Queen enthroned beside;
He had not slept for countless years—
    To lull him scores had tried.

Jack doffed his goose a-feather'd hat,
    A courtesy most clear;
And with a flourish poised his bow,
    But played with little cheer.

The King's eyes glazed like window panes,
    Whose drapes began to fall;
And over all the shadowed court,
    A lethargy did pall.

The pale Queen from her throne arose,
    And offered Jack a comb.
'Now tie your truelove's locks with this,
    And lead her to your home.

'But one thing must I warn you, Jack:
    Until you see the day,
Don't look behind to see her face,
    Or she will drift away.'

Behind the throne an aperture,
    And through it Jack did slip;
A hermit met him in the dark,
    And to Jack did he quip:

'My riddle hear, O Fiddler Jack:
    My house without a door,
Its brittle walls would surely crack
    If it should hit the floor.'

And to this test did Jack reply,
    'The answer is quite plain;
I would be telling you a lie
    To say it taxed my brain.'

The hermit lent sly Jack his lamp,
    And Jack crept down the stair;
His blood was sluggish from the cold,
    While fear pricked up his hair.

He passed then to a darkened wood,
    And followed glowing stones;
The lanthorn lit a ghastly pile
    Of ghoulish well-gnawed bones.

A garden lay in front of Jack,
    An iron fence around;
A garden where no roses grew,
    But bramble did abound.

Beneath an elm a woman sat,
    Her face hid by a veil;
She beckoned Jack to sit with her,
    Before him was a grail.

She poured her tea into his cup,
    And then some for her own;
Jack took a sip and tasted blood,
    And heard from far a moan.

Jack staggered from the garden's gate,
    And wandered up a trail.
A woman wept at river's edge;
    He heard her keening wail.

Cleft in the roof of stone a crack,
    And through it there did shine
A single star upon the one
    For whom poor Jack did pine.

'O Myrrha, dear, my only one,
    I've come so far for you;
O Myrrha, bright, my only sun,
    I've won such games for you;

'O Myrrha, pale, my only moon,
    I'll only play for you;
I'll play this song, through nights so long,
    For Myrrha, only you . . .'

Jack braided tight her golden locks,
    And fixed them fast to stay;
He pinned them with the witch's comb,
    And then he turned away.

He hurried up the glowing path,
    And shunned the sounds behind;
The darkness was so inky black,
    He felt that he was blind.

Jack clambered up the many steps,
    And paid the hermit's due;
He dared not glance behind his back,
    Although he could construe.

The King and Queen were fast asleep;
    The gate yawned open wide;
The sky was pink and forebode dawn,
    But still did Jack abide.

From far away a cockcrow came;
    Jack wheeled around in joy;
A single tear in Myrrha's eye
    Did all his hopes destroy.

The mountain cock crowed mountain dawn,
    And Myrrha turned to mist;
An Angell reckoned in his book
    His Sisters' cruelest twist.

Bereft of rhyme and reason's gifts,
    Jack turned back to his green,
Where pixies streamed from out of rifts
    To dance for him unseen.

But Jack just sat upon his rock,
    And let his fiddle lay;
The pixies begged him for a tune,
    But no more would he play.

They cracked the fiddle like an egg
    Upon a cold hard stone;
And then they took the fiddler's arms,
    And rent them bone from bone.

They feasted on his liver's meat,
    And plucked out both his eyes;
They drank his blood like wine so sweet,
    And relished long his cries.

The pixies took the fiddler's head,
    And threw it in the Tay;
And down it drifted very far,
    Still singing all the way:

'*O golden hair, O golden hair,*
I sang for thee, O golden hair.'

The crow

– IX –
Jack, a Key, and Dreame

Jack had been kickin smack for a coupla years afore he found the key. He was nibblin on a dry hunk of bread on the front porch when a crow came a-fluttrin down and perched on the rickety railin. Jack warn't hungry nohow, and gave his bread to the crow, who took it in his witch-sharp beak and, spreadin wings as black as Abaddon's gate, soared up into the angel-hainted sky. On Friday, just as the clock was a-strikin thirteen, the crow came back and dropped the silver key into Jack's waitin hand.

> Jack found himself upon a road,
>   Which wound deep into Dreame;
> And through a wood he idly strode,
>   Until he heard a scream.
>
> 'Unhand me now, you lawless brute,'
>   A woman loudly cried.
> 'Or I shall put a hex on you
>   To make you wish you'd died.'
>
> 'Come to me, wench,' he said to her.
>   'And let me scratch my itch.
> For here I am the only law,
>   And you are but a witch.'

Jack felt he had to intervene,
    A chivalrous demand;
For he was quite the gallant knight
    And flew to play his hand.

He held Y^e Silver Key to Dreame,
    Once used it would be lost;
But he determined not to yield,
    However great the cost.

'Tantivy!' crowed heroic Jack,
    Who wielded then the Key
To open up Y^e Gate of Time,
    A door within a tree.

Before his foe had time to act,
    Jack pushed him in the *hwol*;
The loutish swine fell headlong in
    A hell which ate his soul.

Well, Leah was the witch's name;
    She welcomed Jack to tea.
He went into her house of stone
    Beneath an ashen tree.

'You don't remember me, dear Jack,
    But I remember you;
You took me from my father's house,
    And pledged to love me true.'

'I do not know if that was me,
       Or if another Jack.
But anyway, thanks for the tea;
       I must be getting back.'

'If him or not, I love you still;
       I'll always be your wife.
It matters not if you know me,
       For you have saved my life.

'I give to you my pentangle
       To wear around your neck;
Since for my honour you have fought,
       May luck be at your beck.'

So Jack set out upon the road
       Which led him into Dreame;
And though he'd lost Y^e Silver Key,
       He had another scheme.

"His skin was green, his hair and clothes:
A nightmare come awake."

– X –
Jack in Yᵉ Dreame

1.

Bleak Winter came to Ettinfell;
　　The Drakes all huddled near
The crimson flames, like those in Hell,
　　Whose bourn they all did fear.

The kindred lived by Hexham Town,
　　And Arthur was their king.
His cousin Jack had much renown;
　　His tales they still there sing.

Hear then a tale of tricksome Jack:
　　A most grotesque affair;
He journey'd far into Yᵉ Dreame,
　　And faced great dangers there.

On Christmas Day a giant called
　　Upon Yᵉ House of Drake;
His skin was green, his hair and clothes:
　　A nightmare come awake.

He walked right in without a word—
  At Yuletide guard was lax.
Upon his belt he wore no sword,
  But in his hand an axe:

An axe, an axe, O what an axe!
  It was full nine feet tall.
So spake the king some words of peace;
  He did not want a brawl.

'I bid thee welcome, titan friend,'
  King Arthur said to him.
'Come seat yourself before the fire;
  The hoar outside is grim.'

'I do not fix to bide, my lord,'
  The giant courtly said.
'I ask of you but one small thing,
  That someone take my head.'

'If any now can take my axe
  And cut my head off clean,
My axe is yours, this witch-sharp blade;
  There's none that's half so keen.

'But twelve months hence he then must come
  Into the wood so green,
Where I shall meet him in the stones
  And have a swing as clean.'

Well, Jack did not take kindly to
    The giant's disrespect;
His kin were eating Christmas goose,
    The hall was holly-decked.

He told the giant, 'I'm your man;
    As sure as I am Jack.
Now set your head down on this board
    And let me have a whack.

'I sure could use an axe like that
    To clear away the thorn
That creeps across my patch of land,
    And leaves my britches torn.'

The giant did as Jack had bad,
    And knelt before the board;
He lay his head across the wood,
    And turned his neck to-ward.

Jack swung the axe, a mighty whack,
    And sliced the neck clean through;
The head then rolled across the floor
    Urged on by Jack's worn shoe.

The Drakes hurrah'd at Jack's bold stroke,
    A bowling ball the head.
The body rose to their surprise;
    They thought that he was dead.

The giant put his head back on,
    And opened both his eyes.
'You got a good lick in, Sir Jack.
    I will not tell bald lies.

'And now your head is mine to lop;
    I'll see you in the stones.
I'll see you there a year from now;
    You'll know it in your bones.'

And then the giant took his leave
    Of Ettinfell's warm hall;
The Drakes resumed their Christmas cheer,
    But happy were not all.

2.

A year then passed; Jack's debt came due;
    He struck out for the stones.
He knew not where his path would lead,
    And followed sighing moans.

His footsteps took him to a wood,
    A dreaming wood some say;
He passed beyond the lands we know,
    Where dreamers often stray.

The wood was dark; the wood was old;
    And Jack was sore a-feared.
An owl a-hooted in the day,
    And that was, well, just weird.

He slept outside for two dark nights,
    And listened to the wind.
He thought of God, the Devil too,
    And wondered if he'd sinned.

And on the third day Jack awoke
    All hoary with the frost.
The dawn was gold and very cold;
    Jack in Y^e Dreame was lost.

Then up ahead a tower rose,
    To heavens soaring high.
To Jack it was a welcome sight—
    He'd feared that he might die.

Jack touched the lucky pentangle
    He wore around his neck;
It wasn't near the first of times
    He'd come close to a wreck.

A watchman hailed; a porter came
    To usher him inside;
The manor was so heavenly,
    Jack thought he must have died.

The manor's lord was Galligant;
    He bade Jack sit and eat.
Jack feasted on a rack of lamb
    So fresh it almost bleat.

His lady sat right next to Jack,
    Lætitia, light of hair;
And with her was her grandmother,
    Though she was not as fair.

Enchanted by Lætitia's charms,
    Jack acted like a fool.
If only she could be his wife;
    Alas, but fate was cruel.

That night the lord with Jack did play
    A most peculiar game;
He offered Jack his hunting spoils
    If Jack would do the same.

Whatever Jack might win that day
    Within the manor's wall,
He'd offer up to Galligant,
    However great or small.

3.

When dawn next broke, Lord Galligant
    Rode off with hounds and horn,
While Jack still lay upon his bed,
    And slept all through the morn.

To his surprise, Lætitia came,
    And sat upon his bed;
Pretending that he was asleep,
    Jack blushed a rosy red.

'Why, you could have your way with me,'
    Lætitia purred to Jack.
'My lord is off a-hunting now,
    And won't till night come back.'

'There's nothing more that I would like,'
    Jack answered unto her.
'Your eyes are green like emeralds,
    Your hair perfumed with myrrh.

'But to another are you wed;
    I cannot take your prize,
Although you lie upon my bed;
    I do not think it wise.'

'My lips, my lips, then kiss my lips.'
    Lætitia begged of him.
'If you'll not take what's in my hips,
    At least indulge my whim.'

Well, Jack, he was a gentleman;
    He kissed Lætitia well.
Her lips were sweet, he could not lie,
    And on them he did dwell.

When Galligant came home that night,
    He offered Jack a stag;
He'd killed it on the hunt that day,
    And put it in a bag.

So Jack then had to offer up
 The spoils he'd won that day;
He kissed the lord upon the mouth,
 But why he would not say.

Then Jack and old Lord Galligant
 Agreed to play once more
A game to trade whatever spoils
 The next day had in store.

And once again, Lætitia came
 To offer up her bloom;
Jack turned her down but kissed her twice
 Before she left the room.

When nightfall came the lord returned,
 A boar dead in his sack;
Two kisses did it earn for him
 From poor embarrassed Jack.

Then one last time Jack played the game,
 As once he'd climbed a bean;
Lætitia offered him this time
 Her girdle silk and green.

'Well wear it neath your linen shirt,'
 Lætitia said to Jack.
'And when the giant swings his axe,
 It will repel the whack.'

Now Jack could not refuse this gift,
    And wore it neath his kit;
And when Lord Galligant returned,
    Jack summoned up his wit.

'I've bagged a fox, my dear Sir Jack;
    Now what have you for me?'
'Why, nothing sir, my hands are bare
    As you can plainly see.'

Lord Galligant did raise a brow,
    For he some mischief saw;
He gave Jack's back a mighty slap,
    And let out a guffaw.

'Not even but a single kiss?
    Cotsplut, yours are so sweet.
No matter then; the feast is laid;
    Together now let's eat.'

The next day saw the Yuletide dawn;
    Jack's debt had now come due.
He thanked the lord and lady long,
    And bade them both adieu.

4.

Jack wandered far into Y^e Dreame,
    A forest dark and green;
The shadows there were whispering
    Of secrets long unseen.

He came upon a rushing brook,
    And stopped to take a drink.
And there he saw a hidden path;
    You'll miss it if you blink.

The path led Jack still deeper e'en
    Into the realm of Dreame;
He did not know when he would wake,
    And wanted much to scream.

At last he reached the sacred stones;
    The giant met him there.
And in his hand the nine-foot axe;
    Jack gulped and said a prayer.

The giant's mouth split in a grin;
    His wolven fangs were green.
'It's time to take your licks, Sir Jack;
    My thirsty blade is keen.'

Jack knelt and bared his naked stem,
    A mushroom's was as white.
The giant swung his eager axe;
    Jack flinched then from his fright.

The giant saw that Jack was scared;
    Jack said it wasn't so,
For many giants had he felled;
    His fame did many crow.

He put his head back on the stone;
    The giant swung the axe.
Jack wore the girdle neath his shirt;
    The thought made him relax.

But this was just the giant's test:
    The third time he swung true;
He only nicked Sir Jack's bare neck,
    And didn't cut it through.

'I guess that's it,' then Jack rejoiced.
    'You got your one lick in.
You didn't take my head clean off;
    You only scratched the skin.'

'You kissed me as my wife kissed you,'
    The giant laughed out loud.
'You kept your word and made the trade:
    Of that you should be proud.

'The second day, you kissed me twice;
    I spared a second lick.
You kept your word until the third,
    And then you played a trick.

'That girdle worn beneath your shirt;
    I know about it sure.
I let you taste my axe's edge
    Your lie to underscore.

'And now you may from Dreame awake;
  Your debt to me is paid.
Lætitia sends you her regards,
  And wishes you had stayed.'

Then Jack departed deepest Dreame,
  And walked to Hexham Town;
His tale he told to everyone,
  And won still more renown.

– XI –
Death Came to Hexham

The Weird Balladeer pulled into Hexham Town. He was thirsting for a drink, as balladeers often are, and paid a visit to Y^e Toad and Crow, the tavern at the crossing of ways. He only had a silver groat, which bought him a glass of nut-brown ale. But when he tuned up his old guitar and strummed by the fire, the drinks started flowing more freely, as did the mutton and bread. His music had a spectral quality to it, which was due to the strings of his guitar. Some said they were haregut, and some said they were the guts of a far stranger beast. Well, perhaps it is better not to pry into mysteries, but let them stay as hidden as the Balladeer's face was by the wide brim of his poet's hat with a crimson feather stuck in the ribbon. Just harken to his ballad. Some say it is English and some say Russian. Just then it was being played in a tavern in Hexham Town. Hwæt!

> When Jack came home from fighting war,
> > He found the wheel had turned;
> For while he'd been in lands afar
> > Time'd passed by unconcerned.
>
> The road to Hexham Town was long;
> > The sun beat down white hot.
> And for his service in the war,
> > Two loaves were all Jack got.

He met a beggar on the road,
    Who was more needful still;
Jack gave him one of his two loaves,
    So he could eat his fill.

Then further on Jack met a man,
    Who wore a long grey beard;
He greeted Jack and knew his name,
    To Jack this seemed quite weird.

Now this old man was hungry too,
    And Jack had one loaf left;
He studied it and took his knife,
    And so the loaf was cleft.

Jack wandered on, then doubled back,
    His error to amend;
'I gave the other man a loaf,
    So take this half, my friend.'

The old man said, 'That is most kind;
    You are a worthy Jack.
And for this kindly deed you've done,
    I'll give you my old sack.

'Now this is not just any sack,
    Though it is plain to see,
For things will jump right into it
    When you say *whickety*.

'A-whickety into my sack,
    And thou shalt never starve,
For if you see a goose nearby,
    That goose a-night you'll carve.

'And one more thing I'll give to you:
    A bottle from dark hell;
To scry if Death is standing by
    Just fill it from a well.'

Then Jack a-thanked him for the gifts,
    And trudged on down the road;
There were a couple turkeys there,
    And so the words Jack crowed.

Enchanted then the turkeys flew
    Right into Jack's old sack;
He sold them to an innkeeper,
    Who dined as well as Jack.

The next day Jack came to a house
    Accursed with devil-blight;
The landlord would give Jack the key
    If he could spend the night.

Well, there were devils in that house,
    Who challenged Jack to play
A game of cards as old as Time;
    Jack won to their dismay.

They came at him with sharp-edged swords;
    This didn't worry Jack.
He grinned so wide his face near split,
    And opened up the sack.

A-*whickety* they jumped right in,
    Just as the turkeys had;
Jack brought them to the ironsmith,
    Who pounded them, by gad.

He whacked and whacked and whacked again
    The devils in the sack,
And in a day 'twas nothing left
    But ashes fine and black.

Now Jack had won the biggest house
    In all of Hexham Town;
He lived in it for many years,
    And all knew his renown.

The Balladeer stopped playing, and set his guitar down to take a long draught of his nut-brown ale.

"What about Death?" came a voice from the crowd. The Balladeer scanned the faces, some dark, some pale, some not entirely human. He found the asker of the question, which hung in the air like the various kinds of smoke swirling around the tavern. It was a towheaded waif, not more than six or seven years old. He was barefoot and wore overalls that had been patched so many times they resembled nothing more than a family quilt. Holding the boy's hand was a woman who was barely more than a girl herself. She had tangled hair that ran down her back and eyes as bright as heaven.

Something about the woman was familiar, and the Balladeer wondered if they had crossed paths before. It was entirely possible, for his path had taken him many places since he had bought that old guitar at a pawnshop in Chattanooga. Some of the places were in this world and some of them were not. He wasn't sure in which category Hexham fell. Perhaps a little of both.

"I heard Jack tied him up in a sack," the little boy said, "and hung him up from a poplar tree."

"My, my," the Balladeer said. "Aren't you a well-informed young fellow."

"Ain't many in Hexham who don't know how Jack tied Death up in a sack, mister."

"Well, then," the Balladeer replied, putting his glass down and taking up his guitar again. "I can see I won't be able to skimp on this one. I'll have to sing you the other half."

A palpable thrill rippled through the audience, and all the voices in the tavern fell silent. All but one.

> A few years on some grave news came:
>   King Arthur's girl lay ill;
> Upon her bed all day and night,
>   She shivered with a chill.
>
> Rife doctors came and tried their best,
>   Spurred on by thoughts of wealth,
> For Arthur'd pledged a heap of gold
>   To who could mend her health.
>
> Now Jack he had no need of gold,
>   But had a noble heart;
> He visited Old Ettinfell
>   To practice hero's art.

He filled his vial up from a well
    To see what he could scry,
And near the foot of the girl's bed
    Old Death was standing by.

Well, Jack he had another trick
    A-slung across his arm;
He opened up his hell-sewn sack
    And said aloud the charm:

'A-whickety into my sack!'
    The Giant-Killer crew;
And into his uncanny pouch
    Y^e Reaper sudden-flew.

King Arthur's girl like Lazarus
    Rose up from Death's grim thrall;
And once again Jack's tricksome deeds
    Were renowned by all.

He took the sack with Death inside
    Back to his sprawling manse,
And hung it from a poplar tree
    To stay the final dance.

Well, Jack lived there for many years,
    And many more beside,
Until he took a walk to town,
    Though sluggish was his stride.

He met a woman on the road,
    And she was far too old:
Back hunched and crooked by her years,
    Two hundred six all told.

'Well, I'll be damned,' Jack said to her.
    'How did you get so old?'
'Why, don't you know?' the woman said.
    'Why, haven't you been told?

'Well, some damn' fool's got Death tied up
    And dangled from a tree;
Until he's loosed no one can die,
    From flesh and bone set free.

So Jack went home and thought it through,
    Then climbed the poplar tree;
He took his knife and cut the sack,
    And from it Death did flee.

The ones who lingered died right quick,
    When torn the devil's sack;
And of the ones who died that day,
    The first, they say, was Jack.

There was a thunderous round of applause in Y^e Toad and Crow, and another glass of brown ale appeared at the Balladeer's feet, as if by magic. Putting down his guitar for the night, he partook of the poet's reward. His eyes narrowed beneath the wide brim of his hat as he scanned the crowd for the blond boy in overalls and his tangle-haired mother. But they were nowhere to be seen.

– XII –
Yᴱ Yellow'd Reed

Jack was in the kitchen sipping China orange tea from a bone china teacup with the handle broken off. He was waiting for HER to come home. They had made a pact to kick it one last time before she moved away to Oregon on the first of June. They had spoken in hushed whispers in bed after he had poured his tea into her pot, and had not breathed a word about it since. But Jack knew that she remembered. And he knew that she knew that he remembered.

He should have left the door shut and the mysteries which lay behind it secret forever. But he was a curious sort, and that was his fatal flaw. It was curiosity which had tempted him through the door the first time. And it was curiosity which had led him down the echoing hall and up the creaking flight of stairs. He had stood upon the garret atop of the house on the hill, and watched the sun rise over the crystal spires of the ruined city, the sky shimmering crimson-red, a cacophony of crows cawing the advent of that heroic orb of orange. I AM THE KING!

The front door squeaked open and snicked shut. There was a tinkling of bells and a gentle cascade of laughter.

> Jack entered into Yellow'd Reed,
>   And Leah met him there;
> From Christian mores his mind was freed,
>   Red ribbons in her hair.

They bedded down in sun-warmed mud;
    Pan play'd his pipes near-by.
Jack heard it in his flesh and blood,
    And joined it with a cry.

Into her cup he poured his tea,
    His milky swirling seed;
Then tea for two made tea for three,
    Right there in Yellow'd Reed.

When he was done then Leah rose,
    And danced to Pan's hoar tune.
Who wrote this song I do not know;
    'Tis ancient as the moon.

And there were many pixies there;
    With Leah did they dance.
They called for Jack to join with them,
    And put him in a trance.

With Leah he made love again,
    And this time she came too;
He loved her with his tongue this time,
    Which like a sparrow flew.

Pan's piping trilled much faster still,
    While pixies bestrode Jack;
And satyrs came to slake their lust
    Upon his fleshy back.

Their swaying shook Yᵉ Yellow'd Reed,
    While hares and rabbits fled,
Till spent at last was all Jack's seed,
    And pixies fell a-bed.

At some point Leah slipped away,
    For she had had her fill;
She left Jack there upon his own
    To dance with whom he will.

At last the trilling of Pan's pipes
    Fell silent to their ears;
The pixies, satyrs, and sore Jack
    Were joyful in their tears.

Till up came Dawn, a-flushing pink,
    Just like a maiden's quim;
The pipes struck up and Jack reached out
    To pull a girl to him.

Though this went on for many days,
    And pints of white milk flowed,
The pixies couldn't hold him long;
    Jack had to hit the road.

While he was donning hat and boots,
    Sweet Syrinx came to him,
And gave him pipes of yellow'd reed
    To play a horny hymn.

So if upon a summer's night,
    You hear an ancient tune;
'Tis only Jack a-playing pipes
    To make the women swoon.

      *   *   *

A Warning to Travellers:
  There is a Door inside the Closet
    Across the Hall from the Nook
      Under the Stair
        There it leads
          I know not
            WHERE?

– XIII –
Jack and the Devil

The Balladeer found himself on the road with Jack. It was the road that wound up Old Hex, the same road Zebulon Drake had trod, oh so many years ago. They walked and talked till even came. And then they pitched a camp, their fire burning bright, deep in the darkend wood. Jack asked his friend to play a song. The old man said he would. The Balladeer'd await his life to play this little tune. And now his weird entwined with Jack's beneath a fateful moon.

1.

King Marock was a stone-heart rogue
    Whom Jack once played at cards;
The King was cool as latest vogue,
    His eyes like glassy shards.

Jack only had a single coin
    He'd found lost in the thorn;
But underneath a lucky star
    Young blue-eyed Jack was born.

Well, Jack beat Marock seven times,
    And on his face a grin,
For he was now a richer man
    From when he had come in.

But Marock had another card
    A-hidden up his sleeve;
He staked his daughter's hand to Jack,
    Who if he lost must leave.

But Jack beat Marock one last time,
    Four aces in his hand;
And with a graceful flourish spread
    His cards out in a fan.

Without a word the King stepped out,
    And left Jack with his gold;
But he had pledged his daughter's hand,
    And must his word uphold.

So Jack went hunting for the King
    With Marock for a name;
But no one knew where he might live,
    Their answers all the same.

Until he came to Jack Frost's house,
    Who also didn't know;
But Jack's namesake did know a spell
    To make the ice and snow.

So Jack Frost froze things hard that night,
    And next morn said to him:
'I found a man who knows the place
    Where Marock's girls might swim.

'I froze his beer, so take this charm,
    And touch it to his cask;
The charm will thaw his beer for him,
    And then your question ask.'

So Jack pulled out of Jack Frost's house
    And set out through the thorn,
Until he came upon the house
    Of Sir John Barleycorn.

Jack asked to see the frozen cask
    To with it touch his charm;
And just as fast as it had froze,
    The beer began to warm.

John Barleycorn was tickled pink
    To see his hop-milk slosh;
Jack took this chance to ask of him
    Where Marock's girls might wash.

He tried to sway Jack from his quest,
    But Jack had made his mind;
So Barleycorn gave Jack his wish
    Of how the girls to find.

Jack wandered to the swimming hole,
    And found three girls in there;
He watched them like a fox in thorn,
    All naked but for hair.

Three skins of swans lay on the ground,
    Jack hid one in the thorn;
Not only neath a lucky star
    But artful he was born.

He waited till the girls got out,
    And in the thorn did hide;
The swan-hides were like coats to them,
    And in them they did slide.

Then two of them did fly away,
    And puzzled was the third,
Till Jack walked up and tipped his hat,
    And asked to have a word.

'O give me back my skin right now,'
    The girl with Jack did plead.
'I'll give you back your skin,' he said.
    'In trade for what I need.

'If you will take me to your house,
    Your skin I'll give to you;
And surely as name is Jack,
    I swear my word is true.'

'I cannot take you to my house,
    For then I would be dead.
I like you Jack, so tell you what:
    I'll take you close instead.'

Jack owned that this was reasonable
    And gave her back her skin;
He thought of Marock as they flew,
    And smiled at his chagrin.

They landed close to Marock's house,
    And so began the game;
The swan-girl took a shine to Jack,
    And Leah was her name.

2.

King Marock was not pleased to see
    Jack stride up to his door;
But Marock was hospitable,
    For he was not a boor.

He ushered Jack into the house,
    And served up quite a spread;
Jack thanked the Lord and suddenly
    There was no meat or bread.

The King's eyes glowed like red-hot coals;
    He left as if in pain.
'You mustn't name the Lord in here,'
    Then Leah did explain.

'My father aims to test you Jack;
    He'll give you thorn to clear.
But take the old axe not the new,
    Or you may die, I fear.'

When morning came King Marock bad
    Arch Jack to clear the thorn
Where once his gran had lost her ring,
    Long years ere he was born.

He ordered Jack to choose an axe,
    The first one dull and old;
The second axe was keen and new,
    And of it Jack took hold.

He whacked and whacked and whacked some more,
    But thicker grew the thorn,
Until the heat of midday sun
    When Jack grew most forlorn.

Then Leah came, old axe in hand,
    And offered it to Jack;
Although it was a rusty wreck,
    He tried to give a whack.

The thorn was cleared, and then he found
    King Marock's grannie's ring;
Jack waited till the sun went down,
    To bring it to the King.

'Now, is my daughter helping you?'
    King Marock asked of Jack.
'Why, no she ain't,' then Jack replied,
    His fingers crossed in back.

When midnight struck, sly Leah came
    Into Jack's tiny room;
It had a bed with tattered sheets,
    A floor which craved a broom.

'Tomorrow morn, you will be asked
    To drain a well so deep
Some say it leads to darkest hell,
    Where even devils weep.

'Down in the well a thimble lies
    Lost by my great-great-dam;
King Marock's test is well devised
    To put you in a jam.

'My father then will offer you
    An old pail and a new.
Your life depends upon the old;
    I swear my words are true.'

When Marock offered him the choice,
    Jack knew what he should do;
But he was under Marock's thrall,
    And so he chose the new.

He bailed the well until midday,
    When water flooded out;
It mattered not how much Jack tried,
    His efforts did it flout.

But Leah came to save the day,
    And brought him the old pail,
Which once belonged to Jack and Jill;
    This time it did not fail.

Jack brought the thimble to the King,
    Who grumbled and he cursed;
He looked so very angry then
    Jack thought his head might burst.

The third day brought another test:
    A house for Jack to build
In one short day from out of stone;
    No mason lived so skilled.

Two hammers Marock brought to Jack,
    And old one and a new;
The new one was a heavy sledge,
    The better rock to hew.

And though Jack pounded till midday,
    The rock stayed hard and whole,
Until his Leah came to him,
    And had to save his soul.

Her hammer was a talisman;
    It broke the rock at once.
By witchcraft then a house was raised,
    And Jack felt like a dunce.

King Marock came to see the house,
    Inspected every room:
The doors and windows, everything;
    The sight did make him fume.

Then suddenly the house fell down,
    Like London Bridge one day;
Jack quipped he had to build the house,
    Not that it had to stay.

3.

The next day Marock walked his girls,
    In swan-skins they were dressed.
He asked Jack which one he would take;
    It was a final test.

But he and Leah had conferred;
    She trumpeted and hissed.
Jack picked her and she showed herself,
    And she and Jack first kissed.

King Marock knew it was the girl
    Who'd helped Jack with his work;
And vowed to kill him anyway–
    The thought did make him smirk.

So Jack and Leah stole away
    Beneath the cloak of night;
They saddled horses and come day,
    The two of them took flight.

Then Marock mounted his black steed,
    And chased them far and wide;
But Leah had a bag of tricks
    To make herself Jack's bride.

She dropped a thorn upon the ground,
    And there a thicket grew;
But Marock touched it with the axe,
    And so the thorn withdrew.

Then Leah dropped a little vial;
    From there a river gushed.
King Marock drained it with the pail,
    And still towards them rushed.

Just one more trick the witch had then:
    She dropped a little rock,
And there a soaring mountain rose
    Which Marock's path did block.

He would have swung the hammer then
    To break the mountain down;
But Jack still wore it in his belt
    Of leather worn and brown.

Well, then they rode to Ettinfell,
    Jack and his bride to be;
He wanted to tell everyone,
    Excited as could be.

> But Leah lingered at the gate
> > And asked of Jack one thing:
> Let no one kiss him on the lips,
> > Or woe it would them bring.
>
> Jack's cousin tried to plant a kiss;
> > He had to hold her back.
> But then a dog jumped in his lap,
> > And on his lips licked Jack.
>
> 'What is this news you have for us?'
> > King Arthur to him said.
> 'I can't recall,' then Jack replied,
> > And scratched atop his head.

The Balladeer quit his strumming. The last note lingered for long seconds until it died away in the moonstruck night. Far away, an owl hooted. The deal was done. Jack rolled a cigarette for himself and the Balladeer. They lit up and lay back with their heads against their packs. The sky was filled with tiny diamonds, like a jewel heist gone bad.

"That it?" Jack said. "That's where the story ends?"

"The story never ends. But that's all I know. It's still writing itself. I reckon the rest of it will come to me when it has a mind to."

Jack wondered where the Balladeer got his songs, but didn't ask. A man had a right to his secrets, and Lord knew Jack had plenty. His lips quirked at the thought of saying the Lord's name out loud, how it had made supper disapparate from King Marock's table. Now he'd heard it, the story did seem a mite familiar, like a dream he'd had long ago. King Marock was the devil, wasn't he? And the devil had as many names as the sky had stars. A star flashed across the sky, a streak of red, orange and yellow, like a bonfire on May Eve.

"Did you see that?" he asked the Balladeer, but his friend was already snoring. Jack shrugged. The star must have been for him alone. He made a wish on it. Then he hunkered down under his coat and caught some z's himself. Jack dreamt the rest.

  Jack's wedding day came soon enough,
    In church and all dressed up;
  He'd asked his cousin if with him
    She'd share a loving cup.

  A girl came in, beneath her arm
    A rooster and a hen;
  The wedding guests all craned their necks
    To see what happened then.

  She put the birds upon the floor,
    And dropped a barleycorn,
  Then asked of Jack if he forgot
    The ring that lay in thorn.

  The rooster ate the barleycorn,
    And then another fell;
  She asked of Jack if he forgot
    The thimble in the well.

  The hen pecked at the second one,
    The third one broke the spell:
  She asked of Jack if he forgot
    The house he built that fell.

  The rooster crowed the cræk of dawn, and the dream vanished like the mist over Old Hex.

– XIV –
The Lay of Old Hex

While the Balladeer went off to take a leak, Jack brewed up a pot of tea. It didn't have as much kick as a cup of coffee, but Jack found it woke him wider. He had a feeling he'd need his wits about him. Today was the day he aimed to climb Old Hex.

After he poured the water and started the tea a-steeping, something caught Jack's eye. Something gleaming in the sun. He walked over to a birch tree and reached into a knothole to pull out a silver key.

"Well, I'll be a giant's uncle," he said. "There you are again."

"What you got there, Jack?" the Balladeer asked, just in time for a cup of tea. Jack poured China orange tea into a pair of chipped china cups that had once belonged to his grannie.

"I done found my silver key! Right there in yonder tree."

"Well, ain't that something?" the Balladeer whistled, and strummed his guitar like he was about to strike up a tune.

"I crave a boon," Jack said.

"Name it."

Jack set the key in the hand of the Balladeer, who looked at it wide-eyed, like a fish out of water.

"I'd like you to hold on to it for me. I got business up on Old Hex, and I reckon it wouldn't do to take the key up there with me. Might fall into the wrong hands if I did."

"And if you don't . . . well, I don't want to say it, but—"

"If I don't come down again? Then hang onto it until you find a one who's worthy of it. Will you do this for me?"

The Balladeer knew there was only one answer. "I will."

The two friends packed up their gear and shook hands. The Balladeer was a-feared he'd never see Jack again. But he'd sing about him till the end of his days. Then they parted ways. Jack took the road up Old Hex, and the Balladeer the road back down to Hexham Town. Travelling Jack never looked back, and neither did the Balladeer. Well, maybe just a quick peek.

* * *

The road up Old Hex steeped upwards something considerable. It was autumn time, and Jack got an eyeful of the valley below, which was painted every shade of red, orange, and yellow that you can imagine. Jack drank it all in. He could see Old Ettinfell from there, Hexham Town, and if he screwed up his eyes he could just about make out the little church-house he'd a-growed up in with his Ma.

At last he stood by the mouth of the cave, the lay of Old Hex, who slept inside the mountain and give it its name. Old Hex is real old. A thousand years, or maybe a million. Some say he's as old as the mountain itself, and the mountains in these parts are as old as some stars.

Jack tried to muster up his courage to step into the darkness, but couldn't quite manage it. A part of him wished he'd kept that silver key. He could have opened a door to some dreamland far away and be quit of this whole black business. Well, Jack may have been footloose, but he wasn't one to break his word.

"Howdy-do, Jack. Do you remember me now?"

Jack nodded. It was the swan girl. Who'd brought him the axe to clear the thorn. Who'd brought him the pail to drain the well. Who'd brought him the hammer to split the rock. He remembered everything. She was the mother of his son.

"I surely do, Leah. I reckon I owe you an apology."

Leah put a finger on his lips. Then she put her own lips on them. Jack was filled with fire, with joy and regret.

"You don't owe me, Jack," she said. "I owe you." She opened up her sack and pulled out a hammer. Jack knew it right off. It was the one thing King Marock didn't have when he'd chased him, so when Leah threw the pebble that grew into the mountain, he couldn't break through it. Was that the mountain they were standing on now? Jack had remembered it as being much bigger. But that was long time ago.

Jack took hold of the hammer and hefted it. The handle was short, and the metal of the head was graven with runes and pictures. He'd never noticed them before. He'd been in too much of a hurry. There were tales in that hammer, of the giants and monsters it had killed. If Jack was lucky, he'd add another one before the day was through.

"Take good care of my boy," Jack said. But by then, Leah was gone. It was time for giant-killing. The hammer gave Jack the courage he was wanting, and, strutting like a bantam rooster, he sauntered into the darkness of the cave.

> King Marock lurked inside the cave,
>   And lay in wait for Jack.
> For twenty years he'd dug his way
>   Into this hell so black.
>
> So deep he'd dug he was not sure
>   If he was man or beast;
> Perhaps he was a hungry worm
>   Who on Jack's flesh would feast.
>
> Jack felt his way into the lay
>   Deep in the heart of Hex,
> Which Marock was, or it was him;
>   It does a mind much vex.
>
> 'You've come at last,' King Marock said.
>   'Now as my son-in-law:
> An irony to say the least,
>   Which sticks fast in my craw.'

'No bone with you have I to pick,'
 Jack brightly did reply.
'I won your daughter fair and square;
 Can't bygones now be by?'

'All fair and square you say to me,
 But what about the coin?
Was it not charmed to win the game,
 My daughter to purloin?'

'It may be so. I do not know.
 It was not my design;
Now we are bound by ties of blood:
 Your kin is also mine.'

The wyrm then hissed envemon'd rage,
 Which nearly splattered Jack.
'I'll give you one more chance, my boy,
 To give my daughter back.'

'I see you will not compromise;
 Let's settle then the score.
This hammer shall be buried now
 In darkness evermore.'

And mustering the hammer's shaft,
 Jack gave it a good swing;
It struck the vaulted roof above,
 Which on them it did bring.

King Marock then and Jack were quit
    Of their great age-old feud.
Who won that day I cannot say;
    A draw it was construed.

"*A woman rose with tangled hair
And languid storm-grey eyes.*"

– XV –
The Ineffable Journey of Jasper Drake

1.

Childe Jasper was his father's son,
    The wit-sharp son of Jack;
And as his father ere had done,
    He never once looked back.

He grew up in a disused church
    Beyond the Devil's reach.
Some said his mother was a witch;
    I won't deny this speech.

When Jasper reached his eighteenth year,
    He found a silver key;
Inside a cedar box it was,
    And now a Jack was he.

So Jasper left to make his way,
    Heart pounding like a drum,
And down the road he strode that day,
    To find what dreams may come.

To Ettinfell he came at length,
    Where Arthur held his court;
The sight of Jasper stole his breath,
    And made his words fall short.

'You have your father's face, my boy,
    His clear blue eyes as well;
I hope you will not tread his path,
    For it leads straight to Hell.'

'Well, that is why I've come to you,'
    Then Jasper said to him.
'I have my father's silver key,
    And so my weird is grim.'

'Ah, that is most unfortunate,'
    King Arthur answered back.
'To me is left no other choice
    Than dub you here Sir Jack.'

From that day on, his weird was Jack's,
    The giant-killer's son.
But Arthur sent him on a quest
    Which his redemption won.

'Remember, boy,' King Arthur said.
    'Although you be a Jack,
Your wit is keen so keep it close,
    When circumstance is black.'

'Do not it let your spirit flag,
    Or cause you to dismay,
For with this key of elder craft,
    In Dreame you'll find a way.

'Deep in the Darkend Wood there is
    A door to Deeper Dreame;
There are but only two on Earth:
    The path lies far upstream.'

All Hexhamites live half in Dreame,
    And half on earth we know;
The mountains there are very old,
    And haunted by a crow.

So Jasper Drake set off to find
    This ancient dreamer's door,
Armed only with Y^e Silver Key,
    Which Nature did abhor.

Along the way, he met a man,
    Who wore a long grey beard,
A wide-brimmed hat upon his head,
    A staff with runes most weird.

'How is your faith, O son of Jack?'
    He then to Jasper said.
'Go dip my staff into yon stream,
    And turn the water red.'

So Jasper took the staff and stirred;
    At first his faith was weak.
But soon the water turned to wine,
    The waters of Y^e Cræk.

'I see your faith is strong, my boy,'
    Then Woden said to him.
'Now take these beans as once did Jack,
    And use them on a whim.'

At Hexham Hollow's lowest ebb
    A-trickled yon a stream.
Y^e Cræk some called it; all agreed
    It was the way to Dreame.

There Jasper stooped to take a drink,
    Which was his first mistake;
It was wasn't long until he blinked,
    And fought to stay awake.

He made a bed in velvet moss,
    Y^e Silver Key in hand;
From there he saw the door to Dreame,
    And then the earth a-ban'd.

The door was in the mountain's side,
    And open'd with Y^e Key;
So as his father had before,
    Then entered it did he.

2.

Beyond the door was black as pitch,
    And he a lanthorn found,
Which lit the way, a tiny star.
    A narrow passage wound,

And at this hallway's other end,
    He reached another door;
He turned the knob and saw a scene
    His father had before.

Beyond the door there was a room,
    A man upon the bed,
With moon-white skin and ruby lips,
    He slept as if stone dead.

'Come to me, Jasper,' said a voice
    He heard inside his head.
'There is much room to sleep with me
    Upon my silky bed.

'For I am Hypnos, God of Sleep,
    And this is my domain.
'Now will you enter or retreat?
    Your answer do not feign.'

'I enter, sire,' then Jasper said,
    As bravely as he could;
And though the god was fast asleep,
    He plainly understood.

'So be it, child. Then you must choose:
  A riddle or a gift.
You mustn't linger in-between;
  Your answer must be swift.'

Now Jasper he was sore afraid,
  For riddles did him vex;
Until it dawned on him the gift
  He'd earned beneath Old Hex.

'I hope this gift suffices well
  I offer unto you.'
The beans he clutched within his hand,
  Then out the window flew.

The moonlight streamed into the room;
  Above the stars did shine;
And in a trice a beanstalk grew,
  A tangled twisted vine.

And as his father Jack had done,
  Childe Jasper climbed and climbed;
He climbed up to the starry sky,
  And left the world behind.

At last as dawn began to break,
  He entered swirling mists;
His feet found purchase on the ground;
  He cried from aching wrists.

To Jasper's awe and puzzlement,
    He stood on cobblestones;
He hoped there was a bed nearby,
    On which to rest his bones.

A gentleman came strolling by,
    Faced east to greet the sun.
'Where am I?' Jasper asked of him.
    'Now that my climb is done?'

'Why, don't you know? How very strange,'
    The man, perplexed, replied.
'Why, this is Hexham, sure as eggs,
    Upon my mam who died.'

'Old Hexham Town? It cannot be,
    For I've just come from there;
This city is too old and large,
    And in bald truth too fair.'

'This paradox I can't explain.'
    The old man scratched his head.
'But you may find that in Y^e Dreame
    Some live who once lay dead.'

He courtly tipped his tricorne hat
    And flipped the boy some gold.
'Hie yourself to yonder inn
    To shelter from the cold.'

Poor Jasper, he was tuckered out,
    Dead tired from the climb;
His coin bought him a soft warm bed,
    Which lulled him in no time.

Now when a dreamer falls asleep,
    Where is there then to go?
I do not know where Jasper went;
    That is for him to know.

But when at last he came awake,
    His stomach loudly cried;
He put his pantaloons back on,
    And to the tavern hied.

And in the tavern Jasper met
    A captain old and white;
His ship set sail when broke the dawn
    To banish dark and night.

Old Scratch sat by the captain's side,
    And sneered, 'You have come back.
'I knew if not your father then
    I'd meet you, son of Jack.'

'I'll strike whatever deal you set
    My father for to find.'
So Jasper said to Mr. Scratch,
    Although his soul it bind.

A sigh of joy Old Scratch let out.
    'I ask of you one thing:
Just sign your name in my Olde Book—
    A quill, pray someone bring . . .'

So Jasper opened up a vein,
    And signed his name in blood;
And though he shed a single tear,
    His heart cried then a flood.

A berth he'd won on Scratch's ship,
    Which next day sailed at dawn;
So all that night then Jasper drank,
    And on a wench woke on.

The ship had tattered sails of black,
    And sailed twixt Earth and Nod.
The captain spent his days asleep,
    And this the crew found odd.

But Jasper recognised him as
    A child of Lilith's brood;
He kept the captain's secret safe,
    For not to would be rude.

A fortnight hence, the boatswain called
    All hands to stand on deck.
The blood-red moon loomed in the sky;
    With foam the waves a-fleck.

The first mate stopped by ev'ry man
    To deal to him a card,
Which each one held close to his chest,
    Its face to closely guard.

An ace of spades was Jasper dealt;
    It was his ink-black weird.
And so a shadow fell on him;
    The Captain's form appeared.

'It is a shame to lose a man;
    Alas it should be you;
To pass between the Earth and Dreame,
    A sacrifice is due.'

A dozen hands then Jasper held,
    And heaved him in the sea;
The ship was swallow'd by the mist,
    And left behind was he.

3.

Then someone came to answer all
    Of Jasper's anguished cries;
A woman rose with tangled hair
    And languid storm-grey eyes.

She wrapped herself around him tight,
    And pulled him down below;
His manhood shoved between her legs,
    And in her he did go.

Some witchcraft kept the man alive
    In Neptune's fluent pale;
Perhaps it was the mermaid's kiss
    That let him air inhale.

She loosed her clutch when he set foot
    Upon the ocean floor:
A temple there of onyx hewn,
    A yawning maw-like door.

A coterie of footmen came
    To usher him inside
The cyclopean ziggurat
    Where horror did abide.

A priestess there, she wore a mask,
    Her blasphemy to hide,
Her purple robes with glyphs adorned,
    The Queen a thousand-eyed.

A tentacled monstrosity
    Upon a jew'lled throne sat.
Its face was like an octopus,
    Behind it wings of bat.

The priestess' incantation rose
    Up to a fever pitch;
And Jasper was a sacrifice
    To satisfy the witch.

The creature straddled the poor boy
  To sink him into IT;
In cold embrace he was unborn
  And vanished up her slit.

In slipp'ry deeps then Jasper was
  Enwombed within a shroud;
And in the darkness came a voice
  Which piped up low and loud.

'It is a tangle you are in,'
  The voice to Jasper said.
'Who are you?' Jasper asked of him;
  His mouth felt made with lead.

'My name is not important now;
  I knew your father well.
And now I must lend you succour,
  Or you will go to Hell.

'Y^e Silver Key about your neck:
  Three times may you it use;
You've used it once if facts are straight,
  And do not me confuse.'

Childe Jasper then did wield the key,
  Or should I say Sir Jack?
He turned it in the door he found
  By groping in the black.

And when he turned it water rushed,
    Engulfing him complete.
He tried his best then not to breathe;
    Air never was so sweet.

Then all at once he washed ashore
    Just like a flailing cod;
He found himself upon an isle
    Where dwelt the King of Nod.

4.

A tower loomed, high, dark and strange,
    Upon a narrow hill;
The wind was like a moaning sigh,
    And Jasper felt a chill.

Then to the tower's gate he came;
    An usher let him through.
As Jasper went into the door,
    A raven loudly crew.

The usher led him to a hall
    To meet with Mistress Grey,
Who sat upon a throne of stone
    And did to Jasper say:

'I welcome you into this hall,
    O noble son of Jack;
For you are kindred of the one
    A-called Y^e Shepherd Black.'

A butler brought a crimson tome,
    Y^e Secrets of Y^e Wyrme,
Where Jasper saw his name inscribed,
    A sight which made him squirm.

'Why have you brought me here this day?'
    Then Jasper asked of her.
'Do you intend to put me down
    Just like a lowly cur?'

'Oh, heavens no,' the Mistress said,
    'You are my cousin, dear.
I ask of you a single boon;
    Come closer now to hear.'

While Mistress Grey gave him a kiss,
    A box yawned open wide;
And twinkling there seductively,
    An em'rald was inside.

It was a Greater Key to Dreame,
    Y^e Silver One much less;
By gazing long into its depths
    Did Jasper acquiesce.

Before he could say yes or no,
    To Hexham he returned;
To Ettinfell the stone he brought,
    His knighthood now well-earned.

He set once more upon Y^e Cup
    The Em'rald he'd procured;
And Jasper drank deep of its Wine,
    Redemption now assured.

– XVI –
Jack in the Witch House

Percival Baskerville went looking for the Fisher King and found himself in Hexham Town. It wasn't much of a town, hardly the Camelot he'd imagined. Really, it was little more than a crossroads and a general store. Percival went inside the store in search of something to quench his thirst, and came out again with a tin cup full of water. He sat on the creaking wooden steps and wiped his brow with a filthy silk handkerchief. A grizzled old man took a seat next to him. He wore a wide-brimmed poet's hat with a crimson feather stuck in the ribbon. There was a guitar slung over his shoulder. The musical instrument was battered, but of exquisite craftsmanship.

"Howdy do, stranger," he said, and strummed a few chords. "Ain't seen you in these parts before."

"I've never been here before," Percival replied. "Although I've been looking for it a long time."

"That so, mister?"

"Call me Percival."

"Pleased to meet you, Percival. Folks 'round here call me the Balladeer."

"The pleasure is all mine."

"So what brings you to Hexham? Ain't many that come here that don't have cause to."

"I am a folklorist by profession. And my specialty is Jack tales. Perhaps you have heard of them?"

The Balladeer's face split into a wide grin that was missing a number of teeth. "I might have at that."

Percival regarded his new friend thoughtfully. "Balladeer, did you say? Do you know any traditional songs? Anything off the beaten track?"

"I might know a song or two."

"Can you play one for me? I'd be most interested to hear it." Percival pulled a well-worn journal and a pencil stub from the pocket of his suit jacket.

"I'd be tickled pink. But not here. I reckon we'd best find ourselves a place to spend the night. Then I'll sing you some old songs by the fire. It's a full moon tonight. And a blue one at that."

Percival footed most of the bill, but the Balladeer threw a few coins in. Then they headed down the dry and dusty trail, until at last they arrived an abandoned mill by the banks of a muttering stream.

"Great heavens!" Percival remarked. "What is this place?"

"Old mill house. Once upon a time they called it the Witch House. Till Jack killed all the witches, that is."

The colour drained from Percival's face. "You knew Jack?"

"I might have crossed paths with him once or twice."

"You must tell me everything! I beg of you."

"Now, now, don't put the cart before the horse. Let's cook us up some supper first."

They both agreed the mill was haunted, and neither of them cared to spend the night inside. However, the Balladeer found a cast-iron skillet in the ruins and, after building a fire from the sticks of the poplar wood that they found in abundance, used it to fry up the steaks Percival had purchased at the store. By the time the steaks were consumed, the sun had dropped beneath the horizon, and they opened up two of the beers the Balladeer had in his pack. Percival sipped his sparingly, but the Balladeer drained his first bottle in short order, then started a second.

As soon as the last of the sunlight faded, the moon gained ascendance and filled the valley with an uncanny light. That's when the Balladeer tuned up his guitar and started strumming the strings, which gleamed in the moonlight.

Once Jack a-hunted up some work,
    And stopped by an old mill;
The miller couldn't hire a man
    That devils didn't kill.

Well, Jack said he would work for him,
    And sounded loud his horn,
For once again the millstone turned
    To grind the barleycorn.

Jack ground up all the farmers' corn,
    Until the darkness fell;
And then he shut the mill wheel down,
    Content to rest a spell.

An old man knocked with but one eye,
    Grey whiskers on his chin;
He had a bag of corn to grind,
    And asked the wheel to spin.

Well, Jack was beat, but he was kind,
    And gave the wheel a spin.
He pulverised the old man's corn,
    Now dust where grain had been.

'You did me right,' the old man said.
    'And I'll do right by you.'
He gave a silver knife to Jack;
    The gift was only due.

Jack built a fire upon the hearth
    To cook himself some meat;
A black cat slunk across the floor
    Upon her padded feet.

Eleven cats watched from afar,
    Their eyes a-glowing green,
While Jack was frying up his meat,
    Their caterwauls obscene.

The black cat then stuck out her paw
    To try to snatch Jack's beef—
Instead a knife's edge her reward,
    The wages of a thief.

The cat cried 'warrrrr' and flew away;
    The others followed suit;
And in the pan a human hand
    Gave Jack a weird salute.

Come breaking dawn, Jack set to work
    A-grinding barleycorn;
The miller marvelled at the fact
    He'd lived to see the morn.

The miller asked Jack what he'd done,
    And why he wasn't dead;
Jack told him of the thieving cat,
    Who'd lost her paw instead.

And then he showed the human hand,
    Where once had been a paw;
The miller's eyes then opened wide,
    And down did drop his jaw.

Upon the finger was a ring,
    A diamond wedding band;
The miller knew just whose it was,
    And just whose was the hand.

That very morn the miller's wife
    Would not get out of bed;
She'd wrapped herself inside the quilt:
    A fever chill, she'd said.

Well, Jack went to the miller's house,
    And as he thought he saw
The miller's wife had lost her hand
    When it had been a paw.

Twelve witches then were rounded up,
    All women in the town;
Jack locked them in the miller's house,
    And then he burned it down.

The music from the Balladeer's strings faded until the only sound left was Percival's furious scribbling in his notebook. The Balladeer frowned.

"I've heard say that if the songs are written down, they'll ne'er be sung no more."

"So the old woman said to Sir Walter Scott," Percival replied, and snapped his notebook shut. "I am prepared to take that risk. For how else will the tales become known in the wider world unless they are set to print?"

"Don't reckon Jack cottons to being pressed into a book like a flower. He delights in being told in a tale or sung in a song. Like the one I'm fixing to sing right now."

The folklorist's notebook sprang open again. The Balladeer sang his song anyway. He couldn't have stopped himself singing it any more than Percival could have stopped himself writing it down. The Weird Sisters were at work, weaving a truelove knot.

> Now Jack once had a couple kin,
> > Who Will and Tom were named;
> They lived together in a house.
> > Upon some land they'd claimed.
>
> The brothers had a bull a piece,
> > And Jack a little cow.
> And while his kindred worked the field,
> > Jack dozed before the plough.
>
> They didn't give Jack any food
> > And killed his little cow;
> Jack skinned it and then cured the hide,
> > And had meat anyhow.
>
> And when the meat was running low,
> > Jack dragged the hide to town;
> He thought to sell the heifer's hide,
> > But looked more like a clown.

Jack knocked on every door in town,
    From each one turned away,
Until a woman answered one,
    Who then to Jack did say:

'I reckon you can stop the night
    Up in the attic loft.
There is a ted of hay up there;
    It is fair passing soft.'

So Jack climbed up into the loft,
    Then someone else came in;
He was a dandy with a tie,
    Mustachioed and slim.

Jack watched them eat and drink then through
    A knothole in the floor;
A plate of meat and wine so sweet . . .
    Then someone at the door.

The woman's beau hid in a chest;
    Her husband sat to eat.
She served the poor man but a crust
    Of bread without some meat.

Well, Jack could not abide this scene,
    And came down with his hide;
The man asked Jack to sit with him,
    The heifer by his side.

Jack shared then of the old man's bread
    That would not suit a rat;
So then he made the heifer rock
    And cocked his ear at that.

'Oh hush now, you,' Jack said to her,
    His cornshuck-stuffed dead cow.
'I couldn't tell him what you said;
    It can't be true no how.'

'Now, boy, you tell me what she said,'
    The old man said to Jack.
'You said the heifer talked to you;
    So don't now hold it back.'

'Well, Bessie says there's meat and wine,
    Up in the cupboard shelf.'
'Is this true?' the old man roared;
    His wife explained herself.

'My kinfolks come on Sunday next,
    And I was holding back.'
'Well, I'm your kin,' her husband said.
    'I reckon so is Jack.'

The woman fetched the meat and wine,
    And they ate very well.
The old man then got awful drunk;
    He stood and almost fell.

'Your heifer hide I have to buy;
    Now Jack, you name your price.
Whatever you may want from me,
    I'll gladly pay you twice.'

Jack would not sell the heifer hide
    For seven guineas gold;
At last he asked to have the chest,
    And so the hide was sold.

The woman tried to sway her man
    From trading Jack the chest;
Her husband made her shut her mouth
    Before she could protest.

So Jack then took the chest away,
    And dragged it to a well;
He said he aimed to drop it in,
    And then he heard a yell.

'Oh, please don't drop me in the well!
    I'll pay you what you want.'
Twelve guineas then Jack got from him;
    It was a fruitful jaunt.

When Will and Tom saw all Jack's gold,
    They shot their cattle down,
Intended to get rich themselves
    By selling them in town.

But unlike Jack's, their hides weren't cured,
    And black flies buzzed around;
Now no one showered them with gold,
    And laughter did abound.

They came home mad as hell at Jack,
    And dragged him to the creek;
They made him crawl into a sack,
    So things were looking bleak.

The brothers had not brought a rope
    To tie Jack in the sack;
They fought about which one would stay,
    And so they both went back.

They set a log upon the sack
    To keep Jack stuck inside.
And in a while someone came by;
    The wriggling broke his stride.

'Who is in that sack,' he asked.
    'A-squirming like a snake?'
'Oh hush,' said Jack. 'And leave me be.
    'I ask for heaven's sake.

'For heaven is where I aim to go;
    'The angels promised me.'
'Oh please,' the old man begged of Jack.
    'I am near ninety-three.

'My hundred-head of sheep is yours
>   If I can go instead.'
> He got into the sack for Jack,
>   And soon the man was dead.
>
> Well, Will and Tom found Jack at home,
>   And they could hardly speak.
> They asked Jack where he'd found his herd;
>   He said inside the creek.
>
> So Jack tied Will up in a sack,
>   And pitched him in the stream.
> His brother Tom soon followed him;
>   Poetic did it seem.

The scribbling of Percival's pencil kept rhythm to the music, and the Balladeer wondered if it wasn't meant to be. Maybe it was time for Jack to be known in the wider world. Jack liked nothing more than to be talked about. There was no denying Percival shared his love of Jack. The Balladeer had never seen a zeal to match. Maybe his time was coming to a close. But not just yet. He still had a song or two left to sing.

"Jack the Giant-Killer," Percival said. "Do you know that one?"

"Jack and the Giants?" the Balladeer replied. "Sure as eggs are eggs. I know it."

"Can you sing it for me? I must hear it!"

The Balladeer stroked his beard and stared into the flickering flames. He had to stave it off. Just a little while longer. "It's a mite late. I reckon I should sing you that one in the day." He had an idea. "I'll sing it to you tomorrow up on Old Hex." The notion gladdened him and he grinned like someone who knew a secret.

"Can't you sing it tonight?" Percival asked. "Or at least start it?"

"Not until tomorrow. But I'll sing you another to tide you over. Just one more. This one ain't about Jack, not directly. It's about a cousin of his. Tamsin was her name. This here's a ballad about her." Percival found himself interested despite himself.

> Fair Tamsin came to Ettinfell,
>   Where bode Josiah Drake;
> She dreamt she'd fallen into Hell,
>   And wish'd that she could wake.
>
> Josiah was a gentleman,
>   And served her tea and cake.
> His manners polished as one would
>   Expect of those of Drake.
>
> He told his guest to fear him not,
>   Although he shunned the light;
> It was a curse upon the Drakes,
>   His ancient family's plight.
>
> They lingered over midnight tea,
>   Though drink he never would,
> And Tamsin feared he more desired
>   Instead to taste her blood.
>
> And after tea Josiah led
>   His comely guest to bed;
> She would not let him lie with her,
>   For fear she would be bled.

The dawn then broke and she awoke,
    Her innocence intact;
And Tamsin roamed Old Ettinfell,
    A manor house in fact.

Josiah dozed inside a crypt,
    Where slept the line of Drake,
Although unlike his other kin
    At night he would awake.

The house was grand but very still,
    As sullen as a tomb;
The poor girl felt a prisoner,
    Ensorcelled by the gloom.

She waited till the twilight came,
    Josiah then returned;
He asked to share her bed again,
    But still his suit she spurned.

And when the daylight came again,
    Josiah skulked away;
He always was a gentleman,
    And would not with her lay.

The second day sly Tamsin found
    A book that told her how
To slay a vampire with a stake,
    And planned Josiah's bow.

She found a knife and made quite sharp
    A poster from her bed;
She waited for the night to fall
    To strike Josiah dead.

She asked him now to come to bed;
    Her pillow hid the stake.
And when he sank his fangs in her,
    She finished off the Drake.

Josian turned to hoary ash,
    And Tamsin took his place;
Old Ettinfell she made her home,
    And youthful still her face.

The Balladeer heard a snore. Percival was fast asleep. The old man covered him with a coarse blanket, and then got forty winks himself.

– XVII –
Jack and the Giants

The two new friends set about rekindling last night's fire to make coffee. The Balladeer recovered an old coffee pot from the wreckage of the mill house and they filled it with coffee from a tin Percival had purchased at the general store.

"Why, Jack himself could have made coffee in this pot," Percival remarked.

"He may have done," the Balladeer said.

Once coffee and some day-old cornbread were consumed, they struck camp and kept on down the trail, which sloped upwards sharply as they climbed Old Hex. As the day wore on and the sun blazed overhead, Percival felt as if he were being boiled alive in his tweed suit. But there was nowhere else he would rather be. The valley spread out beneath him, bounded on either side by low ancient hills like the shoulders of sleeping giants who stood sentinel on this sacred place.

Finally, at midday, they stopped at the mouth of cave about halfway up the mountain. The Balladeer sat down and rolled himself a cigarette. Percival looked into the impenetrable darkness of the cave and shivered despite the heat.

"Shall we keep going just a little further before stopping to rest?"

"Naw," the Balladeer said, striking a match with his fingernail and taking a deep drag of the fragrant purple smoke. "This is where we want to stop. This is where I'll sing my last ballad."

"My dear chap, don't say that. I'm sure you have many years left to you."

"Ain't nothing I can do about it. A man can't escape his weird. I've made peace with it. I've seen things precious few ever dream of. It was a life worth living. Rare as a hen's tooth."

"I won't sit by idly and allow you to . . ."

"Are you going to listen to my song or not?" The Balladeer was already tuning up his guitar, his devil's gift with its haregut strings.

Like a good soldier, the folklorist mustered his notebook and stood his pencil at attention. The Balladeer nodded. For a moment there was silence, only the endless cacophony of cicadas. Then he began to play a song about Jack, the oldest one. Jack and the Giants.

> In days of yore a giant dwelt
>   Just over yonder hill;
> He ate up ev'ry Englishman,
>   And then their blood would swill.
>
> And 'fee and fie and foe and fum!'
>   The giant loud would roar;
> His hunger all the English feared,
>   This giant, Blunderbore.
>
> Well, Jack was but a little thing,
>   Not more than just thirteen,
> A-hunting him a job of work.
>   For times back then were mean.
>
> He walked all day in scorching heat,
>   Up to Old Ettinfell.
> The King was sitting on the porch,
>   And asked Jack bide a spell.

They sat a while and smoked their pipes,
    And drank the mountain in,
When Arthur said he had some work,
    And cracked the widest grin.

'Around the mountain's other side,
    A kin of Ettins dwell;
I know you are the very man
    To send them all to Hell.'

At these words Jack dropped his pipe
    And picked it up again.
'Well, I'm your Ettin-feller, King,
    By heaven and amen.'

'For every head,' King Arthur pledged,
    'I'll pay a pound of gold;
Now come inside and have some lunch,
    Before it gets too cold.'

The Queen served Jack some chicken wings,
    With milk and apple pie;
And in a leather pouch he slipped
    Some rations on the sly.

He took a little hatchet by
    A pile of wood out back.
'That's all I'll need to do my work,'
    Crowed brave and clever Jack.

Then Jack set out into Yᵉ Thorn,
    And climbed up in a tree;
He clambered high to look around,
    And see what he could see.

Before too long the giant came,
    Called Blunderbore by name;
Jack hailed the monster with two heads
    And played a risky game.

'Why, I can squeeze milk from this rock,'
    Jack bragged to Blunderbore,
And cut a slit into the pouch
    He'd stored some milk before.

The giant then picked up a rock,
    And squeezed it in his hand,
But didn't find a drop of milk,
    Instead was only sand.

Emboldened by this victory,
    Jack moved in for the kill;
He cut the pouch beneath his shirt
    And let his supper spill.

Now Blunderbore to Jack exclaimed,
    'Hur, I can do that too!'
He stuck a knife into his gut,
    And so himself he slew.

Jack raised the little hatchet then,
    And chopped the necks clean through;
He took two heads to Arthur's house
    To claim the gold, his due.

But there were still four giants left,
    The Ettin's freakish brood;
Jack couldn't beg off killing them
    Without appearing rude.

So Jack jumped back into Y^e Thorn
    And took his little axe,
A-looking for the giant's kith
    To give their necks some whacks.

Before too long two giants came,
    Just like their murdered kin;
Jack stuffed his pockets full of rocks
    And in a log climbed in.

One giant to the other said,
    'Bore's killer must be grim;
A thousand little Englishmen
    Could not have outfought him.'

They hauled the log that Jack was in
    To use for firewood;
Jack chucked a rock right at one's head,
    And smacked his noggin good.

'Why did you throw a rock at me?'
     The angry giant said.
'I never threw no rock at you . . .'
     'You did! Right at my head!'

Emboldened by his stratagem,
     Jack threw another one;
It clocked the giant on the bean
     And caused hot blood to run.

Then as the giants quarrelled more,
     Sly Jack let fly a third.
One giant pushed the other down;
     A fatal fury stirred.

The giants fell into a heap
     And knocked each other cold;
Jack crawled out with his little axe
     And claimed their heads for gold.

But there were still two giants left
     That Jack had left to kill;
So once more he jumped in Y^e Thorn
     And climbed the highest hill.

A giant named Old Thunderdell
     Came looking for his sons;
Now this one had four frightful heads
     And weighed a hundred tonnes.

He asked Jack to his house to eat,
    A meal cooked by his wife;
Jack followed him back to his house,
    A-fearful for his life.

The giant's wife asked Jack to sit
    Upon a wooden board;
He couldn't help but notice that
    It slanted ovenward.

But Jack kept rocking back and forth
    And falling off the shelf,
Until the giant woman showed
    Him how to sit herself.

As soon as she was sitting down,
    He tilted it up quick;
The giant woman fell for Jack's
    Incendiary trick.

Old Thunderdell was much a-feared
    That Jack would kill him too;
A giant-killer that day born:
    'Tantivy!' brave Jack crew.

'A thousand men the King will send,
    Or maybe two or three.
Get in this chest and hold your tongue,
    Or worm-food will you be.'

And while the giant quaked in fear,
    Jack tossed the chairs and bed;
At last he opened up the chest,
    His enemy misled.

'King Arthur's men are gone for now;
    Leave Hexham while you can.'
Old Thunderdell made haste from there,
    Outwitted by Jack's plan.

When Percival finished scribbling down the words of the ballad, he looked up and saw that another had joined their company. The stranger held a long staff of ebony and wore a black monk's robe, with the hood drawn over his head to obscure his face. The Balladeer stilled his strings for the last time.

"Right on cue," he said.

"Is there nothing I can do?" Percival asked.

The Balladeer shook his head. "The deal is done. Old Hex is only collecting his due. But I have a keepsake for you." He pressed the silver key into Percival's palm. Then the Weird Balladeer allowed the Black Shepherd to lead him into the darkness of the cave, nevermore to be seen.

– XVIII –
The Hexham Horror

Upon the death of her grandfather, Tamsin Willowe inherited a cedar chest containing the most extraordinary collection of journals. And tucked into the binding of one of them was a key.

> *This is the silver key*
> *to the house that Jack built.*

Percival Baskerville had once been a folklorist of some stature, known mainly for his study of the folk-tales and balladry of the Appalachian backcountry. For the last two decades of his life, however, the once-respected academic had been confined to the care of the Powhatan Sanatorium, his work all but discredited.

Tamsin's mother preferred to sweep the embarrassment of her father's disgrace under a carpet of genteel respectability, and his name was never spoken aloud in her house. Needless to say, she had little use for the musty relics that had been the folklorist's few remaining possessions, and the journals had fallen into Tamsin's fastidious care. She alone of Percival's descendants treasured his memory, for they shared a love of the ancient and the bizarre. The journals kept Tamsin company though a painfully introverted childhood, when many a night, alone in her bedroom with only a flickering candle flame for illumination, she pored over her grandfather's sloping script.

> *20th August 1890. Hexham, North Carolina. I have been tracking a most peculiar strain of folk-tale, variants of the 'Jack'-tales so popular in this region of the Appalachian Mountains. These stories are rooted in the*

pre-literate days of heathenry, and hint at foul abominations lurking just beyond our waking perception. These legends are inextricably intertwined with the subject of these tales, who is traditionally named Jack. Jack is the silver key that opens the door to this perception.

After years of wandering the byways that interlaced the borderlands of North Carolina, Kentucky, and Tennessee, Percival Baskerville had stumbled upon a mist-shrouded valley that was not charted on any map. Tamsin vowed that when she was old enough, she would visit this place for herself.

In Hexham it is whispered that a curse winds like a crimson thread through the many generations of Jack's descendants. This is the house that Jack built: Old Ettinfell, the House of Drake.

The chance came when Tamsin's father presented her with a brand new Model A roadster for her eighteenth birthday. She barely waited a week before making the drive from Richmond to the hills of western North Carolina. She wondered what the journey had been like in her grandfather's time, how he had been jostled in mule-drawn wagons and walked for miles on end in the unrelenting summer heat. But once Tamsin started driving on bumpy mountain roads, she found herself suitably jostled, Model A roadster or no.

In the late afternoon, she stopped in a town called Harmon to refill the car's supply of petrol, which had run perilously low. The lean man in overalls who manned the filling station ran a grease-stained hand over the car's shiny bonnet.

"That's one fine automobile," he said in the nasal whine of Appalachian hill-folk, so unlike the sugary drawl of high-born Virginians.

"Well, it ought to be," Tamsin replied. "My father paid a pretty penny for it."

"Now, what's a nice young girl like you doing a-driving a fancy automobile way out here in hill country?"

"I'm on my way to Hexham."

The man nearly dropped the chaw of tobacco he had tucked inside his cheek. "Hexham? What in Sam Hill d'ye want to go to a place like that for?"

"I'm following up on some folkloric leads discovered by my grandfather a number of years ago."

"Girl, if you know what's good for you, you'll turn that fancy automobile around and head on back to wherever it is you came from. Nothing good can come out of going to Hexham."

"I thank you for your concern, sir. But I am resolved. Now please allow to me pay you and I'll be on my way."

As Tamsin placed a dollar bill and three Mercury dimes into the man's calloused palm, something about his manner softened. "Why don't you at least spend the night? I'm sure my wife would be happy to have you for supper. And we have an extra bed. At least wait till morning. You don't want to be heading into Hexham at nightfall."

"That's most kind of you, but I really must be on my way." Tamsin cranked the ignition, and the motor sputtered to life. As she pulled away, she heard him mutter something to himself about *them inbreds up at Hexham*.

To her dismay, the Model A ground to a halt some time later and, despite her best efforts, refused to start up again. Tamsin's mechanical knowledge was virtually nil, and as twilight encroached and the darkness deepened, she regretted not taking up the filling station attendant's offer. But what was done was done, and her thoughts turned to finding shelter for the night.

Tamsin disliked the idea of abandoning the car by the side of the road, but had little choice in the matter. The swaying pines beckoned her into their company. As she followed a trail leading up from the road into their midst, the daylight dissipated and was replaced with the pale glow of a full moon, which gained ascendance over the forest.

Tamsin clutched her tweed jacket tightly to herself, but could not stop her teeth from chattering. After wandering down the path an indeterminate distance, she came to a secluded graveyard a-flower with ancient slabs of slate worn smooth by centuries of rainfall. Tamsin stopped at one of the headstones and ran her fingers along an intricate carving of a skull sprouting flowering shoots. *As you are now, so once was I. As I am now, so you will be.*

She felt comfortable here, as though she belonged in the company of those who lay sleeping beneath the earth. At the heart of the graveyard, ensconced between two weeping willows, was a tomb surmounted by a coat of arms depicting a two-legged wyrm with an erect bearing and a haughty mien.

To Tamsin's surprise, the marble door to the tomb swung open, an invitation for her to enter. Who was she to spurn such a summons? The interior of the tomb was suffused in darkness, but by the moonlight which trickled in through the door, she found a lanthorn containing the waxy stub of a candle. By judicious use of a Lucifer match she found in her pocket, she was able to coax it to sputtering life.

She descended nine steps into the sepulchre, which contained rows of coffins within marble recesses, each coffin containing the remains of one of the family interred there. There was one recess that held no coffin, yet had a name inscribed above it: TAMSIN. The dead were calling their kindred back, pulling her into their fold like a lost sheep.

Tamsin climbed into the hollow recess. It made a comfortable resting place. She bundled up her jacket to serve as a pillow and extinguished the candle. She should have been cold, but her body was warmed by visions of an ancestral fire that had burned in a hearth long ago. She drifted into deep slumbers, and dreamt of a house———————————

> *This is silver key*
> > *that opens the oaken door*
> > > *to the house that Jack built.*

Tamsin turned the silver key in the lock and entered into the interior of the house, which smelled faintly of strawberries. She was awakening to the knowledge that her former life had been the dream and that this was her real life now, here in Old Ettinfell, the House of Drake.

> *This is the silver key*
> > *that opens the oaken door*
> > > *that guards the mahogany hall*
> > > > *in the house that Jack built.*

She walked down the echoing mahogany hall until she came to a library.

> *This is the silver key*
> > *That opens the oaken door*
> > > *that guards the mahogany hall*
> > > > *the leads to the vaulted library*
> > > > > *in the house that Jack built.*

It was far grander than any library she had ever seen, with bookshelves soaring on mahogany wings towards a vaulted ceiling adorned with paintings of angels, a moon, and stars. A mere glance at the shelves revealed a litany of quaint and forbidden titles. But there was one book that especially attracted her attention, a tome bound in a sumptuous shade of crimson leather. She moved towards it and reached for it with her outstretched fingers.

> *This is the silver key*
> > *That opens the oaken door*
> > > *that guards the mahogany hall*
> > > > *the leads to the vaulted library*
> > > > > *that keeps the worm-eaten book*
> > > > > > *in the house that Jack built.*

"I see you admire my books."
Tamsin wheeled around, her face turning a shade of crimson itself.
"I didn't mean to startle you."
The man was deathly pale and wore an azure dressing gown, whose tattered hem skirted the floor like a silken monk's robe. His face was young, barely older than Tamsin's herself, but his eyes were sunken orbs in their sockets.
"Are you hungry?" he asked. The table was mysteriously set for tea, although Tamsin was certain none had been there a moment before. Nevertheless, she consumed the clotted cream and blackberry jam-

slathered scones without compunction, for she had eaten nothing since her breakfast. Her host did not eat anything himself, and sat in his chair, as impassive as an alabaster sphinx.

Finally, her composure restored, and a bone china teacup in her hand, Tamsin introduced herself. "My name is Tamsin Willowe of the Richmond Willowes."

"A pleasure to make your acquaintance, Miss Willowe. I am Josiah Drake." He took her hand in his own and kissed it. His lips were as cold as ice.

"There are Drakes in my family," she blurted out, suddenly remembering it herself. "On my mother's side."

Josiah's lips quirked. "Of that I have no doubt. We Drakes recognise one another. There is something in the blood. A certain quality to the features." He closed his eyes and paused. "But you must be tired. Would you care to stay the night? We can speak more of our shared family history tomorrow. Although not until evening, for I am accustomed to rising late."

Josiah led Tamsin to a room which contained a four-postered bed draped with a swath of gauzy linen. Tamsin was very tired, and the bed offered her sweet solace. But Josiah lingered at the door.

"You needn't sleep alone," he whispered in her ear.

"No," she replied, blushing. "I would prefer it."

Josiah bowed. "Then I shall bid you good-night, cousin." He retreated into the darkness and was gone. Tamsin sank into the soft goose feathers of the bed, and, despite her misgivings, fell fast asleep in moments.

The next morning, she awoke and found herself alone in the house. As Josiah had warned, he did not emerge until after dusk. Tamsin took the opportunity to explore the sprawling manse. There were rooms in Old Ettinfell that defied description. One appeared very small from the outside, but by some illusion stretched on so far that she could not reach the far wall, no matter how long she walked. One room was a shrine, and upon the altar was a horned god with ridiculously large gentials. She backed out of that room very quickly. There was one room that contained a Roman-style bath, complete with fluted columns and a mosiac floor depicting a naked goddess of great beauty. She felt the water with her fingers. It was hot. The prospect of taking a bath was appealing, but she would not allow herself to succumb to the temptation. There was much that was unknown in this house. She wasn't ready to let her guard down yet.

Inexorably, the hall led Tamsin back to the library, where Josiah awaited her with more tea. Night had fallen. She had not realised how hungry she was until she smelled the freshly baked scones. Josiah watched her eat in silence as before, not partaking in food or drink himself. Once again, the crimson book drew Tamsin's eye. Its binding stood out from the other grey volumes like a chiaroscuro. She resolved to read it tomorrow while Josiah slept.

"I have delved into my genealogical records. Might I enquire: was Percival Baskerville your grandfather?"

Tamsin almost choked on her tea. "How did you know that?"

Josiah did not answer her question, but asked another. "His mother was a Drake, was she not?"

"Yes," Tamsin said. Like any good Southerner, she was conversant with her lineage. "Wilhemina. Her father was John Drake. Of the Drakes of Ashe."

"Your Drakes and mine derive from a common line," Josiah said. "Blood calls to blood. It is how you were drawn to this house. It has brought you here."

"I am fatigued," she said, no longer able to bear his company. "I would like to retire now."

"Of course," Josiah replied. He escorted her back to her room, and said breathily, his cold lips brushing her earlobe, "You need not sleep alone."

Despite her revulsion for him, Tamsin found it difficult to refuse his request. His gaze held her in his thrall. But she steeled herself and broke away from him. "Thank you. But I would prefer it."

Josiah may have been a monster, but he was a gentleman. He bowed, and slunk away into the shadows of the hall. Tamsin closed the door, and pulled the covers over her head. She was not able to sleep until dawn.

When she woke, it was already midday. She hastily attended to her toilet and dressed herself. There was only one thought in her mind: the crimson book. It had become an obsession for her. She could see it when she closed her eyes. She longed to hold it in her hands. A few minutes later, she stood in the library, on the brink of attaining the object of her desire. It was only then that she hesitated.

What was in this book? What would happen to her if she opened it? Was it an act that was irrevocable? But the lure of reading its pages was too great. Tamsin could not resist the impulse to pluck it from the shelf, like a beautiful red rose. Savouring the moment, she opened the cover and gazed upon the frontispiece to behold a woodcut of an angel, whose face was hidden by a veil. The image filled her with a nameless dread, and she quickly flipped away from it. Her fingers found a well-worn passage that had been read habitually in the past.

> *Concerning the Thyrſe, commonlie called Thyrſties or the Thyrſtie Ones: knowe that they are diuided into Kyndreds of lyke bloode. Amoungſt these are Hamptown, Drake, Llunwy, Ruſte & Scratch.*

Tamsin heard a creaking sound and for a heart-stopping moment feared that Josiah had awakened. But no, it was impossible. Watery sunlight still trickled into the library through the sunlight. She turned her attention back to the book.

> *Onlie two methods are knowne for diſpatching a Thyrſe. The fyrſt is to ſharpen a ſtyck of holie woode (oake, aſhe or thorn is beſt) & plvnge it with aplombe into the blackened chamber where once a heart had beat. The ſeconde is to part the hede from the bodie by cvtting cleane the neck.*

The clock chimed six, and a grim scheme formed in Tamsin's mind. Reluctantly closing the crimson book, she replaced it in the empty slot on the bookshelf. Returning to her bedroom, she examined the bed where she had slept these last two nights. Grasping one of the bedposts at the head of the bed, she broke it off. She beheld the stick of wood in her hand. Oak, if she was not mistaken.

The broken bedpost was jagged, but would it be sharp enough for her needs? She had to be certain. Tamsin carried it to the kitchen, where a knife awaited her in a drawer. The knife was more suited to carving meat, but it would serve her purpose. Tamsin hacked at the bedpost until the splintered end came to a sharp point. Then she returned to her bedroom and concealed the makeshift weapon beneath her lace-trimmed pillow.

Tamsin heard footsteps echo in the hall. Josiah had awakened. Fighting to keep her composure, Tamsin returned to the library and sat in her chair. He entered. Her heart beat madly. She wondered if he could sense her agitation. But his visage, as usual, was calm.

"Good evening, cousin," Josiah said. "I trust you slept well."

"Yes, thank you," Tamsin replied. She nibbled on one of the scones, then set it back on the tray, uneaten. They sat in silence for an agonising length of time until at last Josiah escorted his guest back to her room. He reminded her that she need not sleep alone. This time, she acquiesced. She lay fully clothed beneath the covers as Josiah clambered into bed with her. He was also fully clothed, for it was not the usual form of purity that he intended to despoil her of. Tamsin shivered from the cold, for her lover was not alive and robbed her body of heat rather than providing it. The last of the Drakes embraced her, and she shrank away from his kisses. But she did not push him away. Rather, she found herself aroused. She had never shared her bed with a man before. Tamsin succumbed to his thrall, her body responding to his. It was only when his thorn-like teeth penetrated her neck that she remembered her purpose. As her life's blood ebbed from her body, her fingers found the sharpened bedpost beneath her pillow. With the last of her strength, she plunged it into Josiah's breast.

"Alas!" he cried. "My twilit existence comes to an close, as I knew it would. Now eternal darkness shall fall upon me. It is well. It is well."

And then his lifeless form collapsed on top of her, a mummified corpse. She pushed him off herself and fled the blood-defiled bed to huddle in the corner, half-naked and alone. Then it occurred to her that she could read the crimson book at her pleasure. All Old Ettinfell was hers to possess. It had claimed her. She was its mistress now, the Lady Drake.

Tamsin found a much grander bedroom upstairs, with a vanity and a wardrobe full of velvet gowns. There was a crimson one which fit her just so, one that must have belonged to another Lady Drake long ago. She brushed her hair, which had attained a silky lustre, and gazed at her face, which was paler than before, her features more refined.

For many days she lingered in the house, reading the strange charts and alchemical symbols in the crimson book until the shapes were etched into her brain. Or was it weeks that had passed? Time moved sluggishly now. Day faded into night and blended into day again. But she shunned the daylight now and preferred instead to wander the halls by candlelight and bask in the moonlight which bathed the garden. The moon appeared to breathe, to beat like a heart, growing larger and smaller, larger and smaller. She lost track of how long she had lingered there. Had it been months? Or years?

Slowly, inevitably, as ivy creeps up a wall, Tamsin fell sway to the thirst. She ignored it for as long as she could by reading books, trying on dresses, and exploring the endless secret spaces in the house. But the need overcame her in the end. She knew she would have to appease it.

And so, when the moon was new and there were abundant shadows in which to cloak herself, Tamsin struck out from Old Ettinfell and walked down the road to Hexham Town. The name conjured memories of her grandfather's journals. She wept wormwood tears that he had lured her into this nightmare from which she could never awaken. There was only one thing that would quench the burning inside her, as hot as the fires of Hell.

He came: the hunted, loping down the road like a fat rabbit in a black suit. It was a drunkard, staggering home after a night at the tavern. Tamsin sympathised with his need to drink quart after quart of nut-brown ale. But that sympathy would not stop her from drinking *him* like a flagon of the finest Burgundy wine. It was as natural as breathing, sink-ing her teeth into his neck. He was enthralled by her and didn't resist in the slightest. Well, perhaps he flailed a little, as the last of his life's blood drained from his body; but the struggling did not last long. Within minutes, he was nothing more than a desiccated husk by the side of the road, while Tamsin slunk back into shadows, a spectre, returning once more to dwell at Old Ettinfell, to dream in moonlight and read the crimson book again and again and again.

Her life passed in cycles of grisly regularity. Some vestige of humanity remained in her, but the thirst was too strong to resist for very long. When it fastened upon her, she had no choice but to strike out into the darkness and hunt her prey. The crossroads proved an admirable place to lie in wait, for those who entered it at night were wayward and unwary. She drank the blood of a milkmaid her own age, who tasted of honey, and a fat man in an ostentatious waistcoat. He was savoury, like a roast pork. And once, just once, she drained the blood of a scrawny boy of seven or eight who had run away from home. She tried to stop herself, but the thirst was too strong. It was then that she knew she had become every inch the monster Josiah had been.

Years passed. She had no way of knowing how many. Time had no meaning anymore. Life had no meaning. There was only the crimson book and the thirst. Sometimes she wondered if the Hexhamites knew that the horror they all whispered of lurked in the ruins of Old Ettinfell. If they did, they were far too frightened to come near it. The house was like a blind spot for them, a terrible secret that haunted their nightmares, but was never spoken aloud. It was a curse that had lasted many generations now. Tamsin had dwelt there for nearly a century and craved nothing more than oblivion.

Then came the sound of footsteps clattering in the mahogany hall. A young man wearing tattertorn overalls and a battered hat swaggered into the House of Drake. He had blond hair and a lopsided grin. It was Jack, the very one whose tales her grandfather had recorded with such enthusiasm. Tamsin now was nothing more than a skeletal monstrosity in a mildewed velvet gown. The thirst was aroused in her. His blood smelled so sweet. It was much more alluring than anyone else's she had yet encountered. She advanced on him, unable to stop herself, though the last remnant of her former self struggled against beast she had become.

Jack did not waste time finding a way to defend himself. He was a giant-killer after all. Out of the corner of his eye, he caught a glimpse of a blade. There was an axe mounted on the wall. It was dusty, but still had a keen edge. He wrested it from its mount and brandished it in front of him. Tamsin managed to speak, her first words in ninety-nine years: "Kill me."

Jack set his jaw. Then he swung the axe in a graceful arc that lopped her head clean off. Tamsin's head rolled across the oaken floor like the ball in a game of ninepins. Her face was young again and at peace. Jack kissed her on the cheek and took the silver key, which dangled from a leather strip looped around her severed neck.

"Tantivy," he whispered. And so was slain the Hexham Horror.

* * *

This is the house that Jack built.

This is the green garden
      behind the house that Jack built.

This is the white rose
      that grew in the green garden
      behind the house that Jack built.

This is the white rose
      that bloomed in the prickly bush
      that grew in the green garden
      behind the house that Jack built.

This is the treacherous maiden
      who plucked the white rose
      that bloomed in the prickly bush
      that grew in the green garden
      behind the house that Jack built.

This is Jack who with his tender thumb
      took the white rose
           from the treacherous maiden
      who plucked the white rose
      that bloomed in the pricky bush
      that grew in the green garden
      behind the house that Jack built.

This is the sharp-pointed thorn
    that pricked the tender thumb
    that took the white rose
        from the treacherous maiden
    who plucked the white rose
    that bloomed in the prickly bush
    that grew in the green garden
    behind the house that Jack built.

This is the red drop of blood
    that was spilt by
    the sharp-pointed thorn
    that pricked the tender thumb
    that took the white rose
        from the treacherous maiden
    who plucked the white rose
    that bloomed in the prickly bush
    that grew in the green garden
    behind the house—

This is the blood that Jack spilt.

– XIX –
The Ballad of Harold Gloom

Childe Harold Drake lived in the gloom
    Of shadow'd Yellow'd Reed;
His habit kept him in a room,
    A craven to his need,

Until the day a Stranger came
    Who bore a Silver Key;
To Ettinfell was Harold heir:
    The last of Drakes was he.

So Harold crept from Yellow'd Reed
    To claim his only due;
And when he saw a garret's crest,
    A raven from it flew.

Y^e Silver Key unlocked the door
    Just as his gran had crooned;
He felt the tumblers in the lock
    As to the House he tuned.

A cold November wind then stirred
    The dried and fallen leaves;
His footsteps echo'd in the hall
    And under hushful eaves.

A jar of Woden's honey sat
    Upon the table top.
He made a pot of tea with it;
    His fingers could not stop.

Into his cup he poured the tea,
    Y^e Ancient Tea of Dreame;
And Harold slumped into in his chair,
    Just as a corpse might seem.

And here began Childe Harold's Dreame
    Upon a creaking stair,
Which led up to an oaken door
    That opened to despair.

Beyond the door a garret lay,
    And here a writing desk;
Upon the desk a crimson book,
    Its contents most grotesque.

In Latin deeps and shoals of Greek,
    He found an English shore;
And in these words he learned the weird
    Y^e Sistren had in store.

Y^e Silent One is conjured by
    A rune which opens Hell;
So take ye up a goose's quill
    And draw then what I tell.

The first line is an inch in length,
    A line of blackest ink,
Upon a sheet of sheerest white,
    A-thirsting for a drink.

A sharpened quill lay on the desk,
    With vellum virgin white;
So Harold dipped his quill in ink
    And worked by opal light.

Adjacent draw one seventh and
    An inch another line,
And measure with a compass arc
    Degrees to twenty-nine.

The third another seventh long,
    The fourth and fifth as well,
And when ye make the sixth black stroke,
    A mark you are from Hell,

For when ye draw the seventh line,
    Two inches full in length,
An Angell shall be summon'd forth
    Whose Silence is a strength.

Childe Harold found himself adrift
    In dark and utter fear;
Y^e Angell wrapped him in her arms;
    And Silence did he hear,

Until he came to rest beside
>   A cold and trickling stream;
Y^e Angell fell away from him
>   And stranded him in Dreame.

A black wood beckoned Harold in,
>   The trees were stark and bare;
He heard an owl hoot in the night
>   And scurried like a hare.

A cold wind blew between the trees
>   In darkness swallowed whole,
With nowhere else for him to turn,
>   Into a cave he stole.

He found in there a maid enchained,
>   Queen Evoë her name;
He freed her with Y^e Silver Key
>   And play'd into her game.

She led him through the winding thorn,
>   Where lay a castle keep,
And sang a lilting lullaby
>   To put his fears to sleep.

A dæmon flow'r bloom'd in Y^e Thorn,
>   A rose at summer's end;
A raven cawed like Roland's horn
>   And doom it did portend.

Childe Harold to the tower came;
    Y^e Silver Key he turn'd;
The third turn was the last he could:
    This from his gran he'd learn'd.

He sat upon an onyx throne,
    And Evoë did bring
A glass of blood-red ruby wine
    With which to toast the King.

Inside a cedar box there lay
    An Em'rald dark and green,
Set once upon an Angel's crown;
    To earth did it careen.

'I bid thee keep this nest-egg well,'
    To him his Lady say'd,
Then locked the gate behind her and
    Into the mist sashay'd.

– XX –
The Devil's Lanthorn

O hear my tale, a tale of Jack,
    Though not a noble one;
Not brave or good, but Jack he was;
    His wit shone like the sun.

Though bright his mind, his soul was black,
    The drunken lazy sod,
And greedy too; I understate
    To say that he was flawed.

The inn where Jack was wont to drink
    Was called Y^e Toad and Crow;
It stood in gloom by crossing roads,
    Suffused in orange glow.

The alewife would not draw for Jack
    And left his tankard dry;
In legendry his debt is sung,
    No comet soared as high.

On Hallow's Eve, a hobhoulard
    Came sidling up to Jack;

He introduced himself as Scratch,
    A gentleman in black.

'If you can turn into a coin,'
    Said Jack, 'to buy my drink,
'To you I then shall sign my soul
    And use my blood for ink.'

'Why, nothing could be easier,'
    Said Scratch to seal the deal,
And turned himself into a coin
    Of gold and cold to feel.

But then Jack pulled a fast one on
    Old Scratch, the wirrikow;
Instead of paying for a drink,
    Jack went back on his vow.

He pocketed the golden coin
    That had a satyr's head;
And in Jack's pocket was a cross
    That filled the imp with dread.

'Oh, let me out,' the boggart squealed.
    'Oh, tell me what you want.'
'Quite simple, sir, just leave me be,'
    Said Jack, insouciant.

Well, twenty years then came to pass,
    And by an apple tree
Jack crossed paths with the nicknevin,
    Who cackled long with glee.

'You thought that you were rid of me,
    But I just had to wait;
For such a man as lazy Jack
    Cannot outrun his fate.'

'I see you have outwitted me,'
    With twinkling eye said Jack.
'Before I go I crave a boon:
    An apple for a snack.'

So eager was he for a soul,
    The hell-wain climbed the tree,
Which Jack ringed round with crosses and
    Then smiled to hear his plea.

'Oh, save your breath,' Jack cut him off.
    'I'll offer you a deal:
I'll let you down if you will pledge
    My soul to never steal.'

'The deal is done!' then screeched an owl,
    Who hooted in the day;
Jack let the clabbernapper down
    And each went on his way.

XX. The Devil's Lanthorn

In course of time, Jack's days were done—
    To Summerland he strode;
But Hemdale laughed right in his face
    And sent Jack on the road.

At length he found the Gates of Hell,
    Where Satan spurned him too;
A mawkin hissed and harpies shrieked,
    And fetches at him flew.

'If Heaven will not let me in,
    And Hades hurls me out,
Where shall I go?' lamented Jack,
    Now racked with fear and doubt.

'Into the dark,' the Devil crowed.
    'But I'll do you a turn;
That rusty lanthorn lying there—
    With witch-fire shall it burn.'

So if you wander in the night
    Into Y^e Yellow'd Reed,
Beware the Devil's Lanthorn's light—
    In it your ruin's seed.

– XXI –
The Ballad of Jack Drake

1.

Jack's mother died on Hallowe'en
    When he was twenty-three;
An heirloom she bequeathed to him—
    A tarnished Silver Key.

But this was not just any key;
    It was Y^e Key to Dreame
A treasure long held by the Drakes,
    A curse though some it deem.

It was not long before Jack's weird
    Was in blackletter spelled,
For he was of the tainted blood
    Of him who Ettins felled.

In Harvard Square, Jack met a man
    Who tendered him some beans;
He took the hoary wizard's gift
    And stuffed them in his jeans.

Though Jack had not a silver dime
    To make an even trade,
A necromantic deal was struck
    That cast his soul in shade.

But Jack had not a lack of wit—
    He knew the beans made five;
And if the Devil asked to dance,
    He'd do his best to jive.

There was a house upon a hill
    In old Jamaica Plain,
On Cranston Street; the angles there
    Could drive a man insane.

That night in bed Jack jabbed a vein,
    An August night and hot;
He split a grain with Leah Drake,
    Who gave his arm a shot.

The needle slid into his skin,
    A sharp and pointed tooth,
Which in his eyes became a key,
    And so it was in truth—

A Silver Key, a vampire's kiss,
    A key into a tomb;
Jack strode into a graveyard then
    Where he would meet his doom.

He found a tomb which called to him,
    An ancient crumbling crypt;
And in it was an oaken door,
    Engraved with strange old script.

Y^e Silver Key slid in its lock,
    Which Jack turned with aplomb,
And stepped across the threshold where
    To Dreame he would succumb.

Beyond there lay a catacomb,
    Engulphed in pitchest black;
Into its reach Jack boldly went
    And never once looked back.

In course of time, the underground
    Gave way to open air;
Jack walked upon a muddy road,
    Although he knew not where.

The road then crossed another way,
    Beside which stood an inn;
Y^e Toad and Crow the place was called,
    Where many paths begin.

Jack had no coins to buy a drink,
    Or anything to eat;
But then he saw a violin
    And fiddled up some meat.

He had the tavern tapping feet
    And caught the courtly ear
Of one who wore a scarlet coat,
    Who beckoned Jack come near.

'My name is Percival,' he said.
    'I reckon you are Jack.'
'Why, that I am,' then Jack replied,
    Though somewhat took aback.

'There is an ancient prophecy
    Writ in a crimson book
That Jack would fiddle down the moon;
    I knew you with a look.'

'Shoot, I ain't nothing special, sir;
    I'm just a country boy;
I think you play me for a fool
    To snare me in your ploy.'

'I give my word, a gentleman
    I promise you I am;
When morning breaks come ride with me
    And see it is no sham.'

But Jack was wise to what he was;
    He was just being coy
And let his patron rent a room,
    The wily country boy.

The barmaid came to ride Jack's horse
    That night beneath the moon;
And by her moans and throaty cries
    He knew she would come soon.

2.

When morning broke there came a knock
    Upon Jack's oaken door;
The barmaid hid beneath the sheets
    Lest she be thought a whore.

Jack struggled into pantaloons
    To meet his courtly friend,
And cast an eye back to the bed
    Where end had joined with end.

The knight asked him to come downstairs,
    Where breakfast now was spread;
Jack welcomed it before the ride—
    He hungered like the dead.

And after he had eaten well
    Of eggs and salted ham,
He rolled a smoke and said aloud,
    'I'm Jack; oh yes, I am.'

Sir Percival lent him a horse,
    A grey and dappled steed;
He had a white one for himself,
    And soon they picked up speed.

A most peculiar sight they struck,
    Side by side the two:
One scarlet cloaked, a gentleman,
    The other's hat askew.

But long they chattered on their ride
    And called each other friend,
Until they came to Ettinfell,
    Which was their journey's end.

Old Ettinfell, that storied house,
    Which once a Jack had built,
Was said to store a cache of gold
    From many giants kilt.

Jack's scions then were called the Drakes,
    For their vast treasure hoard
Was like a dragon's in a cave,
    Defended by a sword.

The Elder Sword of Ettinfell,
    A treasure on its own:
Mercurial and ruby-set
    Upon a hilt of bone.

King Arthur was the manor's lord,
    A king of great renown;
His many deeds were oft retold
    By those in Hexham Town.

Sir Percival brought Jack to him
    To bow and bend a knee;
The gracious king told him to rise,
    So he Jack's face could see.

'You are the one the crimson book
    Foretold was sure to come;
A thousand years and one have passed,
    And pricking is my thumb.

'A quest I charge of you, Sir Jack—
    A knight I dub you now;
And at my table e'er a chair,
    If you will take a vow:

'A Tower stands atop Old Hex,
    And to it must you go,
As surely as your name is Jack,
    And there a slughorn blow.'

'Thy will be done,' Jack answered him,
    And so was struck a deal;
Sir Jack and good Sir Percival
    Sat down and ate a meal.

That night in bed, Queen Jennifer
    Paid Jack a secret call,
And though her husband was his king,
    He fell beneath her thrall.

Her skin was milky as the moon;
    Her lips were scarlet red;
Together they a voyage launched,
    And tempest-tossed the bed.

3.

Ere dawn arose she crept away
    To veil her wanton sin,
For Jack's was now the second key
    She'd to her gate let in.

That misty morning Jack embarked
    With Percival beside;
Together on a thorn-hemmed road
    Fell silence on their ride.

They rode into a dark cold wood
    And soon encroached the night;
And yearning for their warm soft beds,
    They feared the ebbing light.

Then Jack descried a steeple's tip,
    Which peeked out from the thorn;
And though the path was overgrown,
    They now felt less forlorn.

The thorn obscured a small white church,
    Deserted long ago,
And in its windows' coloured glass
    Were pictures all would know:

Miss Muffet and her spider there,
    Jack Horner and his plum,
Cock Robin and Sir Tiny Tom,
    No bigger than my thumb.

Jack's key unlocked the church's door,
    Which, squeaking, opened wide;
And curious, he poked around
    And found a book inside.

Sir Percival fell fast sleep
    Upon an creaking pew,
Beneath a jumping stained-glass cow,
    Who o'er a full moon flew.

Jack found a patch of moonlit floor
    To read the musty book—
A Mother Goose he saw it was;
    He opened it to look:

A house was built by tale-told Jack,
    Who bequeathed a key;
To Deeper Dreaming now he fell,
    A stormy ink-black sea.

He washed upon an island's shore,
    A gloomy sapphire land—
The Land of Nod in legend called;
    Jack stood upon its sand.

And at the island's heart a hill,
    Atop it stood a hold;
This darkend Tower housed a Cup,
    Which bards have sung of old.

Jack started up the winding path
    That led up to the hill;
And as he climbed he clutched his coat
    And shivered from the chill.

Come halfway up the starlit path,
    A garden there Jack found;
The roses long had withered dry,
    But prickly thorn aboun'd.

A woman sat upon a chair,
    Wrapped in a purple cloak;
Her hat was high and conical,
    And then to Jack she spoke:

'You seek Y^e Tower and Y^e Cup,
    Which wait atop Old Hex;
But I am here to tell you now,
    The gate will sore you vex.'

A cocky smile played on Jack's lips
    As he produced Y^e Key;
'That gate will be as maiden's legs,
    And open up for me.'

'Nay, not for thee, my foolish Jack,
    Although I hold you dear;
To only him of purest heart
    Will e'er Y^e Cup appear.'

And then Y^e Tower disappeared,
    The object of his search;
And spinning through the inky void,
    Jack woke up in the church.

4.

Another day arrived and Jack
    Had hardly slept a wink;
Or rather he had waked in dreams,
    Which is the same, I think.

Sir Percival then split with Jack
    A loaf of day-old bread;
Jack wished he had a cup of tea
    With which to clear his head.

They started on the trail again,
    Which led them nearer still;
By midday they were almost to
    Y^e Tower on the hill.

The winding path sloped sharply up
    Their horses slowed and balked.
Dismounting then, in single file,
    In silence then they walked.

At last they reached the very top—
　A heap of stones there loomed;
Y^e Tower where Y^e fabled Cup
　Inside was long entombed.

And as the woman had foretold,
　Jack's Silver Key was spurned;
No matter how he tried his hand,
　The lock could not be turned.

Beside the gate there hung a horn,
　And Jack then knew his part;
He gave Y^e Key to Percival,
　For he was pure of heart.

It opened for the scarlet knight,
　Who stepped into the gloom;
Jack pondered all the twists of fate
　Y^e Sistren loved to loom.

And pressing horn to scarlet lips,
　Jack blew a tantivy:
A signal heard all Hexham wide—
　Tantivy! Tantiveeeeeee!

Y^e Tower came a-crumbling down—
　They fell, the eldritch stones;
And as he had with Jill before,
　Jack tumbled, breaking bones,

Until he woke back in his room,
    And puked upon the floor—
Y^e Silver Key a needle now,
    To Hexham nevermore.

The grimalkin

– XXII –
The Grimalkin's Curse

Jack brushed the ash of nine hells from his coattails. He had fallen from the sky into a thornbush right in the middle of Cambridge Common. But the miracle had gone unnoticed by the throng of tourists snapping pictures of the Washington Elm. They did glance curiously, however, at the overalls-wearing man calling "tantivy!" as he shoved his way through their midst. He slung a canvas sack over his shoulder like some hillbilly Santa Claus and made his way towards the Harvard T station. The Weird Sisters made sure there was a subway token in his pocket for the turnstile. In any case, he would have had little difficulty in vaulting it unnoticed by the conductor. He was Jack.

Yes, I've already told you his name, but it bears repeating, for he was not just any Jack. He was *the* Jack, famed in phrase and sung in fable since misty days of yore. This was the Jack who had climbed a beanstalk and killed the giants by the wagonload. Jack be nimble, Jack be quick. Jack and Jill went up the hill. Currently, he was riding a subway train over the Charles River, a perspective which gave him a commanding view of the golden dome of the State House gleaming in the red-orange sunset. He revelled in his return to Boston, for this was his home, at least in this life. And he had had many. The screeching train lurched underground once more, like dragon retreating to its lair.

Jack switched to the Orange Line at Downtown Crossing and rode it to Jamaica Plain, where he disembarked and climbed a steep hill to the house which awaited him at the top. He had not visited this house in many years, but it was still just the same. It had doors and windows, many angles and worms in the wood. He turned the key in the lock, and the door creaked open. Jack was home.

The first thing he did was make himself a cup of tea and retire to his bedroom with it. He could check the mail later. Right now he took the cedar box out of the canvas sack and set it on his desk next to the Underwood typewriter. Jack lit an American Spirit to steel his nerves and open the box.

"Well, hello, Jack," said the severed head inside the box. "It's about time you gave me some air. It's a bit musty inside here, you know." The head belonged to an old man with a long white beard and pale blue eyes which stared madly at him. Well, I suppose anyone would be a bit mad, being a disembodied head.

"Do I know you?" Jack asked, the memory dangling just out of reach. He had lived many lives, popping up throughout history like, well, a jack-in-the-box. But he was always Jack. Then it hit him who the head in the box was. How could he forget?

"Why, 'tis I, Ezekiel Whitlock, once minister of the Church of Mother Goose."

"Reverend!" Jack said. "Am I glad to see you!"

"Reverend no longer, I am afraid. But I am glad to see you, Jack. And, as usual, there is much to do. It is time for us to return. Back to where it all began."

"Return? Return where?"

The once-Reverend Ezekiel Whitlock smiled as reassuringly as a severed head could, which was more than you might believe, for he was a most reasurring fellow. "Why to Hexham, of course. Hexham! As sure as eggs are eggs."

Jack and Ezekiel chatted of old times, for once the floodgates were opened, Jack's memories came pouring back. Then he saw a guitar case in the corner of the room. Funny—he'd never noticed it before. Opening the case revealed a beautiful black guitar. It smelled of attics and old books. Jack propped the guitar on his lap and started strumming it, filling the room with redolent magic.

"Why, Jack," Ezekiel said. "I didn't know you knew how to play."

"Neither did I."

A stream of silver moonlight flooded the room and Jack remembered a song which was as old as the hills. He had become the Weird Balladeer and the Weird Balladeer had become him. Or perhaps he had always been. Fiddle-dee-dee. The Old Ones were, the Old are, and the Old Ones shall be. "This one's called the Grimalkin's Curse," Jack said. And he began to sing.

> King Arthur dwelled in Ettinfell,
> >   An ancient oaken hall;
> And if you asked in Hexham Town,
> >   He was a king to all.
>
> Now Hexham is a haunted place,
> >   Where devils roam at night,
> Where warlocks, imps and cluricans
> >   Make mischief their delight,
>
> A fisherman once cast his net
> >   In misty old Lake Nod;
> His catch he vowed to sacrifice
> >   Up to the Hidden God.
>
> His haul that day was bountiful;
> >   He couldn't give it up,
> And kept it for himself so that
> >   At night he could well sup.

The second day he vowed again
    To sacrifice his yield;
But once again he kept it all,
    And so his fate was sealed.

The third day dawned quite bleak and cold;
    The mist engulfed his boat;
And in his net a kitten purred—
    Pure sable was her coat.

The fisherman then took the cat
    Back to his small abode;
But soon to monstrous size she grew,
    And scarlet rivers flowed.

The grimalkin lurked in a cave
    That yawned on Hex's slope;
And anyone who strayed nearby
    Abandoned then all hope.

Well, all who dwelt in Hexham bid
    King Arthur show his hand,
For once his forebear Jack had rid
    The giants from the land.

So Arthur then convoked the Drakes,
    His weird-entangled brood,
A wizard too, with pale blue eyes,
    And ancient lore imbued.

Old Whitelocke was the wizard called,
    And none knew whence he came.
He bore a rune-carved staff of ash,
    And ballads told his fame.

This strange and storied kin then rode
    Their horses up Old Hex;
The mountain loomed above so high,
    They had to crane their necks.

There was a single narrow path
    That led up to the cave,
And one by one they rode uphill,
    Their manner very grave.

At last they reached that forlorn place,
    Old Hex's yawning maw;
But of the cat they saw no sign,
    Not whisker nor a paw.

'I'll draw him out,' Old Whitelocke said,
    And blew upon his horn;
King Arthur held a spear in front,
    Just like a rose's thorn.

The grimalkin pounced from the cave
    And batted Arthur's spear;
It snapped in two and then the cat
    Bared fangs, instilling fear.

The horrid beast leapt at his throat,
    But Arthur raised his shield,
Which struck the creature hard enough
    To fall upon the field.

Enraged the monster flew at him
    And, hissing, bared her claws,
Which tore his skin and drew red blood,
    Which caused the puss to pause.

The heinous cat then licked her claws
    To relish a king's blood,
And sneered to see it drip upon
    The cold and common mud.

King Arthur then, enraged, struck back
    For such a vulgar slight;
He drew his sword and raised his shield,
    Preparing for a fight.

The creature tried to bite his neck
    And crush it with grim jaws;
But Arthur held his shield up high
    And snared the hellion's claws.

The clever Drake now hacked her paws,
    Which dangled from his shield;
The grimalkin launched at his chest,
    Too frenzied now to yield.

The hind claws of the cat ensnared
    King Arthur's leather belt;
And two more paws his sword lopped off—
    A death blow at last dealt.

Across all mist-veiled Hexham then
    A caterwaul was heard;
Tantivy cried King Arthur when
    His milk-white horse was spurred.

That day the devil there was slain
    Upon Old Hex's slope;
And Arthur and the Drakes delayed
    Abandoning all hope.

– XXIII –
THE BLACK TREE

Jack awoke the next day at the crack of noon. He wasn't quite sure what had happened the night before, except that it had involved drinking a lot of whiskey and a disembodied head. He moaned and, opening the curtain a crack, was stabbed in the eyes with dagger of sunlight for his trouble.

"Excuse me, Jack."

Jack hurriedly covered his nakedness with a sheet. He was naked? He must have had a good time last night. To confirm it, there was someone else in his bed—a female someone, with raven-black hair strewn across ivory skin. She was fast asleep. Then who had just said that? He scanned the room and his eyes widened when he saw Ezekiel's head lying on the floor on its side by the wall.

"If you wouldn't mind . . . this is a most uncomfortable position."

Forgetting his nakedness, Jack picked him off the floor and set on his desk next to his typewriter. It looked appropriate somehow. Then it sank in. "So . . . last night. I don't remember much, but were you there when we were—" He glanced at the girl in his bed and wish he could remember her name.

"I'm afraid so. Fortunately, I was facing the wall at the time. Although I heard everything."

"Sorry. I was a mite drunk. I don't recall much from last night."

"That much is apparent. Never mind, I've plumbed depths of madness you couldn't even imagine. Last night pales in comparison. Her name is Eliza, by the way."

Eliza. Of course. Some of the night before was starting to come back to him. He remembered an intense conversation with a girl in a bar.

Telling her how he was Jack from the fairy tales, and of all the adventures he'd had since climbing the beanstalk. What an embarrassing play. Not that it wasn't true, of course. He heard a moan. She was stirring.

"Perhaps it would be circumspect to put me back in my box," Ezekiel suggested. "We don't know how receptive the young lady will be to my reanimated state. I suggest we take things slowly."

Knowing good advice when he heard it, Jack gingerly placed Ezekiel's head back in the rune-inscribed cedar box—still blackened from the fires of Hell—and closed the lid just as Eliza's eyes fluttered and opened.

"Well, hello there, stanger," she said, a wry smile playing across her lips. She made no effort to hide her nakedness, and Jack allowed himself to admire the supple curves of her body. If Ezekiel wasn't able to hear everything from inside the box, he'd be tempted to stage an encore of last night's performance, the particulars of which were starting to percolate back into his memory.

"Morning, Eliza," Jack said and risked a kiss of her scarlet lips. She didn't protest. That was a good sign.

"I wasn't sure if you'd remember my name. Say, I'd murder for a cup of coffee."

"Sure," Jack said. "I'll see what I can do. How do you like it?"

"Black."

A few minutes later Jack returned with two mugs filled with hot coffee. Eliza had the guitar on her lap, idly strumming the strings. He liked the juxtaposition of the dark red wood against her flawless white skin. The muse and the lyre. It was time for Orpheus to take the stage.

Eliza set the guitar down carefully and took the cup of streaming black bean juice. "Do you play?"

Jack smiled. "I know a few licks."

"I'd love to hear a song."

He sat on the bed beside her and took the guitar in hand. Jack didn't know what he was going to play, but then it came to him. His harrowing of Hell was already a ballad. It had always been one and always would be.

Jack had lost Yᵉ Silver Key,
    When he was twenty-three;
And twenty more then passed before
    He found it in a Tree.

Although he'd lost Yᵉ Key to Dreame
    Some twenty years before,
Yᵉ Tow'r haunted him at night;
    In days he woke no more.

And so Jack went a-questing for
    A way into Yᵉ Thorn;
And there he met a hooded monk,
    Whose robes were tattertorn.

The Stranger was not hard to find,
    Yᵉ Shepherd and his crook;
He led Jack to a ruined house,
    Which held an ancient book—

A crimson book, a book of worms,
    By many names 'tis known;
Who reads it knows of all the rings
    The Tree of Life has grown;

And far beneath another Tree,
    A shadow to the first,
Yᵉ Tree of Death, its branches bare,
    Its roots for blood a-thirst.

And in the crimson book's dry leaves,
    A Silver Key Jack found;
For though he had outrun his Fate,
    It chased him like a hound.

Before he closed Y^e Booke of Wyrme,
    Y^e Shepherd's hungry tome,
He gazed once more upon the Tree
    For paths that he could roam.

The rotted house in Hexham Wood,
    Old Ettinfell its name,
Was like Y^e Tow'r on the hill,
    Its darken'd stones the same.

And then an urge allured him like
    A puppet, string-enthralled.
Jack wandered deep into the Wood;
    Y^e Shepherd to him called.

A ring of stones beneath the moon
    Jack found hid in the Wood;
Y^e Shepherd waited for him there,
    His face cowled by a hood.

'Well, here I am,' Jack boldly said.
    'I've walked into your snare.
'But know you this, O hungry wolf;
    I am a clever hare.'

The moon above eclipsed, blood-red;
    The Shepherd drew a knife.
Jack looked around in mortal dread
    And feared the end of life.

But death was not the end for Jack;
    The Shepherd cut his palm.
His blood dripped slowly on a stone,
    Which made him strangely calm.

Jack held Y^e Key, his arm outstretched,
    Just like a dowser's wand;
And then the Devil's Blacken'd Tree
    Held forth for Jack a frond.

Jack climbed it as he had in youth
    The beanstalk told in tale,
And left the world of waking men
    To find a hallowed grail.

But Jack was not one pure of heart;
    His soul with stained with sin,
And unlike pilgrims gone before,
    Sharp wit his goal would win.

So Jack stepped through Y^e Shepherd's gate
    And saw the road ahead,
Which wound in coils, a sleeping snake;
    He thought he must be dead.

But death was not the end for Jack;
  It was another gate.
Tantivy was his battle cry;
  He marched then towards his fate.

A lanthorn lay beside the road
  And glowed with witch's fire;
Jack took it up to light his way,
  To make the dark less dire.

He came across a stream of blood
  Of Ettins he had killed,
And heaped beside it giants' bones;
  The sight left Jack's blood chilled.

A dark-eyed man came riding up;
  His horse was raven-black.
'Sam Lee my name, I welcome you,
  O tale-told daring Jack.'

'You flatter me, my fallen prince,
  O noble Duke of Hell.
Your riddles do not flummox me;
  I know you, Samaël.'

'Tread softly, Jack,' growled Samaël,
  'Or I will tan your hide.
Queen Lilith's Tow'r opens now;
  She welcomes you inside.'

A second horse appeared for Jack,
    Milk white with silver bells,
And bore him to an eldritch place,
    Where night forever dwells.

The Tow'r was a cold dark heap;
    Jack sheltered in its stones.
A wretched hag came down the stairs,
    And like the wind her moans.

'Some meat, some meat,' she snarled to him.
    'Your horse you now must kill.'
And like a perfect gentleman,
    Jack answered, 'At thy will.'

And when the monster ate his horse,
    She begged for wine to fill
The horse's hide, which he must sew;
    Jack answered, 'At thy will.'

And when she had the wine drunk up,
    In one long gurgling swill,
She asked him up to bed with her;
    Jack answered, 'At thy will.'

And at the Tow'r's very top,
    Beneath the darken'd stones,
Their love was lit with opal light,
    And like the wind their moans.

At last her passion all was spent;
    Jack strained to keep apace.
He saw his long-absconded wife,
    And youthful was her face.

Then Leah pulled a cedar box
    From underneath her bed;
Jack opened it and found inside
    A severed human head.

But this was not just any head;
    It opened pale blue eyes.
'Ezekiel, my name,' it said,
    While Jack hushed fearful cries.

'Ezekiel is very wise,'
    Smiled Leah then to Jack.
'And if you ever you lose your way.
    He'll help you get it back.'

Then Leah closed the cedar box
    And put it in a sack;
And Jack and she made love again
    Before he turned his back.

Y^e Silver Key slipped in his hand,
    Mercurial the thing,
And like the full moon's beams it caused
    The Bedlamites to sing.

A man arrayed in tattered clothes
    Appeared, his name Mad Tom;
And to Jack then he sang a song,
    As solemn as a psalm.

'I went on down to Satan's mess,
    Where sinners screamed and burned;
He served me up souls piping hot
    That on a spit a-turned.'

So Jack went down to Satan's gate;
    The Black Man stood athwart,
Of noble mien with shepherd's crook,
    Patrician his comport.

'I guard the Gate of Yog-Sothoth—
    What would you ask of me?'
And Jack replied, quite cavalier,
    'To wield Y^e Silver Key.'

The Gate revealed a walled-in place,
    More secret than a tomb;
Jack slipped Y^e Key into the space
    That led into the womb.

And so it was Jack came unborn
    And drifted in a void
That lay between the world we know
    And one the wise avoid.

XXIII. THE BLACK TREE

And in his sleeve, Jack's final ace,
    The head inside the box,
Whose eyes were blue as heaven's cloth,
    And no one could outfox.

'A most peculiar state this is,
    Not dead nor yet alive;
If I were you, my dear friend Jack,
    I'd check that beans make five.'

Inside the pocket of his jeans,
    Jack found the wizard's gift;
And tossing them into the dark,
    The beans gave him a lift.

For even Nyarlathotep
    Could not outthink this plan;
Jack climbed the devil's beanstalk to
    The place where Time began.

And there he found the Tree of Life,
    An apple hanging low;
Instead of innocence instead
    Jack ate and all did know.

Then tumbling like Lucifer,
    He landed in the thorn;
On Michaelmas in Harvard Square,
    Jack blew upon his horn—

> My bold tantivy all ye hark;
> I am Y^e Ettinfell!
> My name of Jack the annals mark,
> For I have harrowed Hell!

Eliza sat staring, her coffee cold, her cigarette in the ashtray burnt to a stub. "I want to fuck you so badly," she said, straddling Jack. The head of Ezekiel Whitlock groaned softly inside the cedar box.

* * *

After making love with Eliza, Jack fell into a deep sleep. And he dreamt.

* * *

Jack found himself in a tangled wood. The trees towered over him. He couldn't not tell if it were day or night. A stream trickled nearby, but he wasn't able to find it, despite his burning thirst. At last he stumbled upon a crumbling ruin, a long abandoned chapel. A lone raven perched upon the steeple and cawed balefully as he approached. The daemon scrutinized him with eyes like shards of black glass. Jack entered the chapel and found the inside as cold as it was outside. But at least it provided shelter from the wind which moaned incessantly in that forest. The altar was bare and had no cloth or chalice. Instead was a silver key, as old as the stars. The Silver Key to Dreams. Jack was being given another chance. On the wall behind the altar was a painting of a woman in a flowing purple gown combing her tangled locks. He knelt at the altar and bowed his head, holding his hat in his hands.

"Didn't take you for the praying type, Jack."

Jack slipped the key into his overalls pocket, then rose and turned about to face the one who had invaded the chapel's sanctity. It was a gaunt man, haggard, and older, perhaps fifty or sixty. He wore a neat moustache, a wide-brimmed hat, and a long black coat that skirted his ankles. Jack said his name: "Marock."

"Glad I made an impression on you, boy. Seeing how I'm your father-in-law, I reckon I ought to have."

"Last time I saw you, you were stuck inside of Old Hex."

"A setback. You'll be seeing me again. Real soon. I'm coming to claim my kingdom."

"Your kingdom?"

"Hexham."

"Arthur is King of Hexham."

"No longer. But you'll find out. Say howdy to Leah for me. Tell her Daddy's coming home."

* * *

Jack awoke next to his lover, who dozed beside him. He opened the curtain a crack and gazed at the moon's reproachful face.

"I'm doing the best I can," he muttered.

"Your best was more than sufficient," Eliza answered him, now awake.

"I have to go back," Jack said.

"Go back where?"

"Hexham."

"Will you take me with you?"

Jack opened his palm and found the Silver Key to Dreams laying in it.

"As sure as eggs are eggs."

– XXIV –
The Death of Arthur Drake

Eliza and Jack got as far as nowhere-in-particular, Pennsylvania, before stopping for the night. Eliza drove a hearse. She was Gothic to the core. Goths weren't exactly known for camping, but she was game. Jack knew what he was going, and soon he had a blazing fire going. And once the fire was started and the stars twinkled coldly in an infinite night, Jack tuned up his guitar and played an ancient ballad on his haregut strings.

> Old Marock is a kin to Drakes,
>   A cousin of the King's;
> A cloak of darkness circumscribes
>   The calumny he brings.
>
> King Arthur and Sir Mordred met
>   Upon a thorny field;
> And when they quit there were two souls
>   In toothy Death's grim yield.
>
> Now on the night before the clash,
>   King Arthur deeply dreamed
> Of sitting on a silver throne,
>   Or so to him it seemed.

The chair was fixed atop a wheel,
    Which then began to turn,
Until he found himself below,
    In Hell where sinners burn.

His wife and kin ran to his room
    To rouse him from his screams;
And so he fell a-slumber then,
    Not waking nor in dreams.

Sir Jack appeared before him there,
    As well Y^e Sistren Three;
And unto good King Arthur Drake,
    Sir Jack then made a plea.

'O do not fight, my cousin dear,
    For death it doth portend;
Nay, stall for time and stave it off,
    Or it will mean your end.'

But Arthur would not take that course,
    For honour he would keep;
And in the morn he faced a foe
    That made all Hexham weep.

At dawn they met at Summer's End,
    A field of rose and thorn.
The king wore white, and Mordred black;
    And Jasper blew his horn.

Two feuding houses battled there—
    The Drakes and Mordred's kin;
They soaked the roses with their blood
    As swords in flesh went in.

King Arthur thrust his spear into
    Sir Mordred's blackened heart;
But in his death he took revenge
    And practised poison's art.

Sir Mordred pushed his body up
    The span of Arthur's spear;
And smote his father in the head,
    When he at length came near.

Sir Bedivere heaved Arthur up
    And staggered to the wood,
Where in a copse of whisp'ring yews
    A mossy chapel stood.

Inside the king was comforted,
    And drew his cousin nigh.
'My Caliburn now take from me,
    For I am soon to die.

'I bid thee cast it to the deeps
    Of mist-obscured Lake Nod;
For when the rose has witherèd,
    The stem belongs to God.'

But Bedivere could scarcely bear
    To lose the jewel-set sword;
And so he hid it in a tree,
    Although it broke his word.

King Arthur asked Sir Bedivere
    What happened at the lake;
The knight spoke only of the mist
    And showed himself a snake.

King Arthur asked a second time
    To cast the sword away,
And once again the knight could not
    And from his path did stray.

At last the king turned crimson-faced,
    And called his knight untrue;
Sir Bedivere then raised the sword
    And towards the lake it threw.

A hand then rose up from the lake
    A woman's, lily-white;
So wan and spectral was its form,
    He quivered at the sight.

King Arthur knew then from his words,
    That Bedivere was true,
And bid his knight to carry him
    To where the raven flew.

> And there upon the gloomy deep
> Of misty dark Lake Nod,
> Three Sistren stood upon a boat
> To take him back to God.
>
> And as King Arthur disappeared
> Into the swirling mists,
> Old Marock stirred in Hex's heart,
> Where evil e'er persists.

Eliza lit an American Spirit and shared it with Jack. They breathed deeply of the purple haze which quickened their minds and shortened their lives.

"So, the Jack in the song," Eliza said. "Was that you?"

"I reckon it was."

"You knew King Arthur?"

"Sure 'nough did."

"That's hot."

"I helped his son out on a quest to win a lady hexed by a warlock. Lopped the devil's head clean off. But that's a story for another time. I'm a mite tired." He put his guitar back in its case.

"Not too tired to fuck, I hope."

"Hell no."

And so they did.

Eliza fell asleep after their lovemaking. But Jack was restless and wandered into the darkened wood. They were at the foothills of the Appalachians, and he could smell home in the trees.

Deep in the wood, Jack found the ruins of an ancient church, overgrown with moss and thorn. The bell in the steeple had lain silent for long years. The sight pierced his heart, for he had grown up in a church just like it, just him and his Ma.

"How beautiful are the daughters of the moon, who play amidst the ruins."

A trio of maidens danced in the moonlight. They were clad in purest white, their skin white and their streaming hair. Pan was playing his pipes, and Jack had no choice but to heed them. He joined the whitewomen's dance, weaving in and out of their reel in a trance, the dance that had wheeled since the beginning of time, the dance that would continue until the end. In the shadows unseen was a shepherd robed in black, his face hidden by a robe, in his hand a staff of ebony. He watched the danced without passion and took secret delight in it. The whitewomen drew Jack closer to them and clutched at his clothes, unbuttoning his shirt with pale fingers, unfastening the straps of his overalls.

"Get away from him!"

The whitewomen shrieked and draw away from Jack, who stood dazed in the moonlight. Eliza advanced, and the whitewomen skittered away, back into the shadows of the forest. The shepherd disappeared along with them.

"Jack? Are you okay?"

"Eliza? Is that you? What happened?"

"I just saved your bacon, Jack. I thought you were the one who outwitted the things that go bump in the night."

Jack cocked a smile, his wits restored. "Who told you that fairy tale?"

Eliza turned to head back to their campsite, but Jack lingered, looking thoughtfully at the ruins.

"Come on," Eliza said. "Let's get back to the fire. This place gives me the creeps."

"You go on ahead. I'll be along directly."

"But what if they come back?"

"Don't you fret none. I'll be right behind you."

Reluctantly, Eliza started back without him. Jack stole into the ruins of the old church and found what he was looking for. It was right where he thought it would be, in a secret chamber of the rotted pulpit. A glass vial filled with dream dust, which sparkled in the moonlight. He slipped the vial in the pocket of his overalls and headed back to the warmth of the fire and Eliza's embrace. And deep in the wood, the black shepherd waited with grim satisfaction, the whitewomen danced macabre, and the moon turned to crimson.

– XXV –
Scarlett Cloake

Jack strode back to find Eliza shivering before the fire. Her eyes were wide with fright, for she had seen beyond the veil for the first time. She had seen mysteries that were hidden to all but the barest few, and now she was one of those scant number. Nothing would ever be the same again.

But here was Jack, with strong arms to comfort here. He was young as nimble and crackling with wit. He stood between the world we knew and the cosmic horrors which stood to wash over it like a tidal wave of darkness. Perhaps he could not defeat them, ultimately, but he was would do his best to stem the tide. He would not go gentle into that night. It was then that Eliza made a vow. Neither would she. She would rage, rage against the dying light.

"Well, I don't reckon either of us are a-goin' to get any sleep tonight."

Jack pulled the guitar out the case. For the first time, Eliza noticed how uncanny it was. The wood was almost black, and the strings gleamed silver in the moonlight. It was an instrument of Hell, she thought. But it kept them safe too, when Jack played it. He was playing the Devil at his own game. Her money was on Jack. He strummed a few chords, and the music harmonised with the sounds of the forest—the moaning of the woods, the whispering of the trees, the hooting of the owls. And somewhere in that forest, the black shepherd listened.

> I sing the song of Scarlett Cloake,
>
>   The gloomiest of girls,
>
> Who dwelt beside Y^e Darkened Wood,
>
>   Her hair in inky curls.

Her beldam span a scarlet cloak,
    Which she was wont to wear,
And so all those in Hexham Town
    Her beauty would declare.

Her mother sent her to Y^e Wood,
    For Beldam now was ill;
She wrapped up in her scarlet cloak
    To keep away the chill.

She bore a basket filled with bread
    And cream so sweet and white,
And whistled olden songs to keep
    Away her mounting fright.

A Black Man loomed where none ere was,
    A shadow-dwelling fiend,
Who watched her with his hollow eyes,
    As on a staff he leaned.

'Where go ye now, my pretty maid,
    Your basket filled with bread?
Why, don't you know this wood is dark
    And haunted by the dead?'

'Beyond the ruined mill there waits
    My beldam's crooked shack;
I heard that she had taken ill,
    And came to bring a snack.'

The Black Man wove a twisty scheme
    To take a shorter way,
And get to Scarlett's beldam's house
    While she was still at play.

'Who knocks three times?' the beldam asked.
    'Is it my Scarlett Cloake?'
'Why, so it is,' the Black Man said,
    And like a girl he spoke.

'Dear, lift the latch; the door will ope;
    And thou mayst enter in.'
A smile suffused the Black Man's face,
    Convinced that he would win.

He rent the beldam limb from limb
    To cook her in a pot,
Then dressed himself in her old clothes
    And in her bed he got.

Now Scarlett knocked upon the door,
    And in the beldam's croak
The Black Man bade her lift the latch,
    So entered Scarlett Cloake.

'I've stewed ye up some meat, my dear,'
    The Black Man sweetly said.
'Avail thyself whilst it is hot;
    'I'll wait for thee in bed.

'Your voice is harsh,' so Scarlett said
    As she sat down to dine.
''Tis but the cold,' the Man averred
    As she drank blood like wine.

And then reluctantly she crawled
    Into that bed so cold;
The Black Man had no mortal life,
    For he was æons old.

When Scarlett Cloake looked in his eyes,
    She saw eternal dark,
And glowing there a dancing wisp,
    A tiny greenish spark.

'What eldritch eyes you have,' she said,
    And shivered in her soul.
'The better you to know how vast
    The cosmos is in whole.'

And now she saw his werewolf's fangs,
    As sharp as winter's thorn.
'What titanic teeth you have . . .'
    And then she heard a horn.

Well, it was Jack's, this tantivy,
    Who burst right through the door,
And swung an axe, his Elder Gift,
    Which nature did abhor.

'Ye shall not claim this soul today,'
　Exclaimed the Ettinfell,
　　And banished Nyarlathotep
　　　Back to gates of Hell.

XXV. Scarlett Cloake

– XXVI –
The Pixy-Wife

All tales end tragically. The only way to have a happy ending is to cut the story short. End it in the middle. Except for Jack's. His story never ends. It just goes on and on. And that is his tragedy. He felt for the vial of Silver Key in his overall pocket as Eliza drove down Route 26 out of Asheville, North Carolina. It was mid-afternoon on a late October day, and the tree burned with spectral fire. Then Jack saw the turnoff, the old sycamore tree, bent over like Old Man Time himself.

"Turn there," he said, just in time for Eliza to swerve onto a little dirt road she would have missed if she'd blinked. "This is the way to Hexham."

In about than half an hour—less time than Eliza had expected—they arrived in a small town nestled in the midst of wild domed hills, which loomed strangely in the distance. They could not ascertain whether or not town was abandoned, but there had a general air of decay about the place and most of the houses and store fronts were boarded up. It there were any residents, they were staying inside and watching them furtively through the cracks of shuttered windows.

Jack told Eliza to stop by a boarded-up general store with an antique gas pump beside it. But the pump was dry and the prices were from another era. A crow fluttered down to perch on the roof of the store, which was boarded up like the others. There was nothing there for them—no song-filled tavern or comfortable bed for the night.

Jack got back in the car and told Eliza to keep driving. They traversed a series of backroads, which Jack guided her down with uncanny recollection. At last, he told her to stop pull the car over by the side of the road. They disembarked. Jack slung his guitar over one shoulder and his sack over the other. Eliza followed in his wake. And in the rapidly fading twilight, Jack led them down a path into the dark wood, which swallowed them up into its depths.

At length, the path led them to an old barn, which had seen better days, but was still standing. Jack opened the front door and peered into the darkness of the interior. It smelled of hay and animals—not unpleasant. It would give them shelter for the night. They set about gathering wood for a fire—the second night in a row—and set it blazing by the mouth of the barn. Jack had some bread and cheese in his sack, which made for a meager supper, but it was better than nothing. At last, Jack tuned up his guitar, and played a ballad. The ancient hills harkened.

> The Drakes who dwelt in Ettinfell
>   Were well endowed with gold,
> Except for Jack, who was quite poor,
>   Though known for being bold.
>
> But being bold was little use
>   When weddings came around;
> And lavish were the wedding-gifts
>   When Arthur's wife was found.
>
> Miss Jennifer was fair of skin,
>   A lady most high born,
> And all the Drakes came to the feast,
>   Save Jack who was forlorn.
>
> He took a walk into the wood,
>   Y^e Shepherd's dark demesne,
> Until he came upon Y^e Cræk,
>   Which thread it like a vein.

The quintessence of pixydom
    Flowed through that murky stream;
And drinking of that water deep,
    Jack found himself in Dreame.

Two pixy-maids in green and gold
    Found Jack there as he slept,
And led him to their lady's house
    Upon which ivy crept.

The lady of that house declared
    To Jack her secret love,
And all the gifts of conjury
    Befalling him thereof.

Y^e Lady Leila was her name;
    Jack revelled in her mien,
In how the moonlight gave her skin
    An opalescent sheen.

They dallied in her bed that night;
    Jack's finger fit her glove,
Until the dawn came drawing near,
    When she cut short their love.

But ere she sent Jack on his way
    A favour she bestowed:
A bag of gold which had no end,
    And like a river flowed.

Another gift she offered Jack,
    Y^e Ancient Silver Key;
She bade him wield it when he may
    If her he wished to see.

Jack never must mere mortals tell
    About his pixy-wife,
Or his words would slice the spell
    As if a whetted knife.

Well, he was loath to leave her house,
    Though leave it so he did,
And ventured back into the world
    As wide-eyed as a kid.

It was too late to celebrate
    The wedding of Y^e King,
But Jack made use of pixy gold
    To buy his Queen a ring.

Returning then back to his house,
    Jack lived a lordly life,
His garments fine and well he dined,
    And visited his wife,

Whenever he desired her;
    He turned Y^e Silver Key
And called Y^e Lady from Y^e Door,
    So joyful they could be.

And when another year had passed,
    Jack's charity was known
To Hexham Holler's furthest reach,
    For far his gold was sown.

A summons came on Saturn's feast:
    A call to Ettinfell,
For Jennifer desired Jack
    His exploits her to tell.

But when they were alone within
    Her dark and shuttered room,
She offered then to show her guest
    The fullness of her bloom.

But Jack refused to lie with her
    And spurned her soft embrace;
He held a more supernal love
    And found her offer base.

But Jennifer was most displeased
    That Jack had spurned her lust,
And used her role as Arthur's Queen
    To sow in him distrust.

She claimed that Jack had come to her
    With amorous desire—
A suit which Jack in court denied
    Most strongly to his sire.

'My heart belongs to one who is
    More fair than she, the Queen.'
So Arthur said, 'Who is this one
    That none has ever seen?'

Quite in a thorny plight did Jack
    This question now ensnare,
For knowledge of his pixy love
    He'd promised not to share.

But Jack was not abandoned by
    His Silver Key-called wife;
The Pixy-Queen appeared to all
    To save her lover's life.

She blew her scorn on Jennifer
    And blinded her blue eyes,
And from the men in Ettinfell,
    Her sight evoked long sighs.

Then Jack and Lady Leila rode
    Upon a milk-white steed,
Until they reached the shores of Nod,
    A misty lake indeed.

A boat await the Queen and Jack
    To take them both to Hen,
But little else is known about
    What happened to them then.

– XXVII –
The Lay of King Marock

Eliza snuggled into Jack's chest to keep herself warm in the infinite night. He was so solid, so real, the only permanent thing in the shifting sands she found herself in. And yet, she knew it was an illusion. Jack was the Trickster himself, alchemical mercury, the quintessence of fickleness. But for now, for this moment, he was here and comforting her. She intended to enjoy it while she could. Jack put his guitar down and stroked her hair while he gazed thoughtfully into the flickering flames. Then he nodded, as if he had come to a descision.

"Eliza," he said, "there's someone I reckon you ought to meet."

Gently disentangling himself from her, he opened up his canvas sack and pulled out the cedar box, blackened with hellfire and carved with Aklo runes. Jack whispered an ancient litany under his breath and then opened the lid to peer inside. Ezekiel's kind blue eyes stared back at him.

"Well, well. I was wondering when you were going to introduce me to your friend."

"Jack?" said Eliza. "Who are you talking to?"

"Keep your wits about you, 'Liza. This is going to be mite unsettling."

Jack pulled the disembodied head out of the box. Ezekiel blinked in the firelight and smiled.

"How do you do, young lady. My name is Ezekiel Whitlock."

Eliza's mouth hung upon, then she snapped it shut, recalling something her mother had once said about catching flies. Pull yourself together, she thought. Yesterday you rescued Jack in the Beanstalk from a swarm of pixies. This was relatively tame on the insanity scale. Nothing to lose your marbles over. Nevertheless, there was something particularly disconcerting about a living head without a body talking and making facial expressions. It was like an animation—like something from a Ray Harryhausen movie.

"Hi," she finally managed to say. "I'm Eliza."

"A pleasure to meet you, Eliza," Ezekiel replied, his politeness unfailing, even in his undead state. "I know my appearance must be unnerving for you. Believe me, it is even more unnerving to be in such a state oneself. Quite literally in fact, as I am missing my entire nervous system."

"Maybe we can find your body," Jack said. "Put your head back on and bring it back to life. Must be a way."

"Tempting as such a prospect is, I feel I should shun the path of necromancy. I shall never regain favour in Mother Goose's eyes that way."

"Aw, nuts to Mother Goose. She's left us all to twist in the wind. I say we go our own way. Left-hand path, right-hand path—both the same to me."

"Nevertheless," Ezekiel said, "I shall continue to pursue my redemption. Although I do fear I tax your kindness by relying on you to carry me around in a box."

"Bedads, don't you fret none about that. You'd do the same for me. Now, wouldn't that be a sight? Then I'd be a honest-to-goodness Jack-in-the-box!"

"Well, we can't just leave you in a box," Eliza said. She folded up a blanket next to the fire and gently rest Ezekiel's head on it. Jack strummed his guitar, as was his habit when he was thoughtful.

"Well," he said, "you told me I had to come back to Hexham. So why are we here?"

"Perhaps you should play the song that's swirling around your head," Ezekiel suggested. "I have a feeling the answer shall be forthcoming."

So Jack did.

Sir Marock was a knight of yore
    Who served King Arthur Drake,
Who from the Ettins in Y^e War,
    A hoard of gold did take—

And with this gold a title bought,
    A barony with land;
He lived there with a baroness
    Inside a house so grand.

But ev'ry month for three long days
    Sir Marock disappeared;
Just where he went he would not say,
    Which struck his wife as weird.

She wheedled him to manifest
    The mystery he held,
Until he told her of his woe,
    Which was unparalleled—

For when the moon was fat and round,
    He took a savage form,
A monstrous wolf who roamed Y^e Wood
    And thundered like a storm.

It was an inbred curse, he claimed,
    Nine generations long,
Inflicted by an ancestor
    Who once had done great wrong.

And when three days had come and gone
    He donned his hidden gear,
To once again take human form,
    Full thirteen times a year.

The baroness was mortified
    To hear her husband's tale
And would no longer lie with him;
    His sight would turn her pale.

And so she met in secret with
    Her lover near the thorn,
And bade him there to hide the clothes,
    Which lately had been shorn.

And when he found his clothes were lost,
    The werewolf loosed a growl;
For he could not resume the form
    He had before his prowl.

Although his servants searched for him,
    Sir Marock ne'er was found;
His wife bestowed the manor house
    And soon in white was gowned.

A year then passed, and in the wood
    King Arthur hunted game
And loosed his hounds upon the wolf
    Who once had Marock's name.

But then a most amazing thing:
    The wolf begged Arthur's grace,
Displaying human gentleness
    Despite a bestial face.

The King then took the wolf from there
    To dwell in Ettinfell,
Though little did he know his knight
    Was snarled in Satan's spell.

When Christmas came all Hexham went
    To Ettinfell to feast,
For nearly all were kin to Drakes,
    Or married to at least.

And when the wolf saw his old wife
    He snarled at her and leapt
To bite the nose right off her face,
    Ere aught could intercept.

Old Whitelocke knew who Marock was
    And questioned hard his wife,
Who then confessed her cruelty
    Before she lost her life.

The baroness returned the clothes,
    Restoring Marock's form;
But nothing could reverse the curse
    That gathered like a storm.

Sir Marock asked Old Whitelocke's help
    To rid him of his curse,
And offered all the gold that was
    Within his leather purse.

Old Whitelocke opened up a book,
    A horrid crimson tome,
Which many had in secret read
    And caused their mouths to foam.

Sir Marock read an eldritch spell
    By Ancient Ones adored,
For it had been contrived by ones
    Whom even Baal abhorred.

And ne'er again did he become
    A wolf in full moon's light;
Instead a dæmon stole his form
    To claim his kingly right.

Jack stopped strumming. Eliza and Ezekiel had fallen asleep. It struck him as strange—no one had even fallen asleep during one of his songs before—but he took it in stride and covered Eliza up with a blanket. Ezekiel was a peculiar sight, a disembodied head lying on the ground snoring. Jack picked him up and placed him back in the cedar box, which he closed.

"Well, well. So now you know my story."

The voice issued from the fire without obvious source. Jack peered into the flickering flames. He failed to divine a shape, but the voice was familiar to him. Marock.

"Is that you, king?" he said.

"I'm coming for you, boy. You promised to build me a house."

"Never promised that it would stay up, though."

"Can't outwit your way out of this one, Jack. I'm almost through the mountain. When I come out, I'm taking back my kingdom."

"Your kingdom?"

"Hexham. I'm the rightful king. Once and future."

"Arthur's King of Hexham."

"Not any longer. He's gone off to Nod. I'm taking his place. You fixing to stop me?"

"I aim to."

"You ain't man enough, Jack. Tell my daughter hello, *son-in-law*. Tell her I'm coming for her too."

The fire flared up for a moment and then returned to normal. The voice was silent. Next to the fire lay a Silver Key. No, it was a needle. Same difference, he reckoned. Jack felt his overall pocket and found the vial he'd stolen from the church. Flakes of moon. He tapped them into a spoon and mixed them up with water. Then he drew it into the needle and rolled up his sleeve. The vein was waiting, throbbing and blue, like a mighty Leviathan. He jabbed it with the needle and shot IT, the pearly white powder that tastes better than chowder, and Jack danced on the moon with the dish and spoon.

– XXVIII –
The Unquiet Grave

Eliza awoke to a cock crowing the dawn. Then the mountain cock crowed the mountain dawn and Ezekiel Whitlock opened his morning-blue eyes. An Angel reckoned a soul in a book and Jack was gone, leaving behind only a black guitar and a silver key. Eliza picked up the guitar and strummed the strings. They resonated at an unearthly frequency, and the spectres stirred in the Darkened Wood. She lay her hand across the strings to silence them and hastily put the guitar back in its case. But she knew the instrument belonged to her now, that it was her weird to sing the ballads from outside of time, the ballads written by an unseen hand. She turned to the disembodied head who was now her only companion.

"Jack's gone," she said.

"When one door closes, another opens," Ezekiel replied.

A lone figure emerged from the wood, tall and lanky. He wore tattered overalls and had stringy brown hair. But it was the eyes, the wide blue eyes, full of curiosity and wonder. Eliza had seen them before.

"Jack!" she burst out, suddenly overwhelmed by the urge to hug him. Then she stopped himself. "Jack?"

"I'm Jack," he said in the soft hesitating voice of one who was unaccustomed to speaking. He looked as if he had been in the forest a long time.

"You're not the Jack I know." It wasn't, yet he seemed so familiar. His eyes. Something about his face.

"You must mean my cousin. He's got the same name as me."

"Well, I'm Eliza." She hugged him anyway. And this is Ezekiel."

"A pleasure to meet you," Ezekiel said.

Big Jack (or so Eliza come to think of him) was unfazed by the sight of a talking head. Instead his attention was fixed upon the silver key lying on the ground. "Pretty," he said. He picked it up and slipped it into his overalls pocket before anyone could object.

Eliza rooted around in the sack Jack had left behind and came up with a pair of apples. She offered one to Big Jack, who accepted it readily enough. He took a noisy bite. Eliza nibbled on hers.

"I wish we had some coffee to go with it," she said.

"There's tea back at the church." Big Jack offered.

Ezekiel's eyes twinkled. "Would you be good enough to take us there, Jack?"

"Follow me."

"Would you be good enough to carry me? I'm afraid I'm not particularly ambulatory at the moment."

Big Jack polished off his apple, core and all, and tucked Ezekiel's head under his arm like a football. Then he trudged back towards the wood. Eliza picked up the guitar case and took a last wisftul look at the ancient manor house brooding in the distance. Is that where Jack went? Why hadn't he taken her with him? She supposed their paths had diverged. He was his own quest and she was on hers. Perhaps somewhere up ahead, their paths would cross again. At least she had friends to keep her company on her journey. Jack was all alone. But that's how he always ended up in the end. How we all do, when we cross that final door, to the lands which lie beyond. Eliza hoped at least that Jack was happy.

* * *

The night before:

Awash in moonlight, Jack stepped up to the great oaken door which guarded the entrance to Old Ettinfell. The house That Jack built.

This is the house that Jack built.

This is the silver key
  To the house that Jack built.

This is the silver key

    That turns the iron lock

        To the house that Jack built.

This is the silver key

    That turns the iron lock

        That opens the oaken door

            To the house that Jack built.

The oaken door creaked open to reveal a mahogany hall. Jack's footsteps echoed as he walked down it. Hung on the wall were murky oil paintings of the generations of Drakes who had lived in this house, the descendants of Jack the Giant-Killer—the Ettin-feller as he was known in the old tongue. Here was Jackson Drake, a haughty look upon his noble visage, resplendently arrayed in magnificent armour as he prepared to bestride his white horse and charge into the mouth of Hell to retieve the star-fallen emerald. But it was Josiah who returned it to the Black Shepherd, to fulfil his father's bargain.

    Jack reflected on the Black Shepherd, how long that old sorcerer had been writing his family's life, ever since he had given Jack a handful of black beans at the marketplace. How much they had cost him—much more than an underfed cow. He was still paying for that trade to this day. If only he could drink from the White Cup, Jack could be free of his entanglement. But how? Every move he took only took him deeper into the darkness. Inevitably, the labryinth of hallways in Ettinfell Hall led him to its heart: the vaulted library.

This is the mahogany hall

    that lies beyond the oaken door.

This is the mahogany hall

    that lies beyond the oaken door,

whose labyrinthine turns led, inexorably,
to the vaulted library.

This is the vaulted library
in the house that Jack built.

There was a skylight high above the vaulted arches. A silver sliver of moonlight snaked its way into the library, like Lilith's finger, and pointed to a particular book on the highest shelf. Jack eyes were drawn to it, and he positioned a ladder to climb up to it as he had once climbed a beanstalk many centuries ago.

He opened it and found the way to the dark tower in a black spell, an ancient spell known by the Old Ones. He stole with the book up to the garret above the House of Drake. There was a skeleton sitting at the writing desk, a quill clutched tightly in its bony fingers. The skeleton was wearing tattered overalls and a battered hat just like Jack's. He pushed the skeleton out of the chair, and the skull rolled across the oaken floorboards like a bowling ball in a game of ninepins. There was time enough for bowls and to outwit the Black Shepherd. Jack took his place at the writing desk and, taking up the quill, dipped it in the black ink and began scratching words into the virgin white vellum by the light of the silver moon streaming in through the window.

* * *

Eliza, Big Jack, and Ezekiel arrived at a white church in the middle of the wood. Eliza was beginning to feel as though the Wood had swallowed her whole, that she would never find her way out. But at the same time, she felt at home here. The most wonderful things had happened to her since she had come here, since she had met Jack. She had crossed over from the dreary grey of the waking world into the colour out of dream. Nothing would ever be the same again.

The church was old and white, with a steeple atop, which housed a bell that once chimed a-Sunday, but had lain dormant for many a year. Big Jack wielded the Silver Key and unlocked the door, which swung open. He made an "after you" gesture to Eliza, who, after a moment's hesitation, crossed the threshold.

The interior was what one would expect of a backwoods church: two rows of pews with an aisle between them. A pulpit presided at the front, and she made her way towards it, the floorboards creaking beneath her boots. It smelled of a million attics, and rays of sunshine shone through the stained glass windows forming rays in the dusty air. She heard the sound of Big Jack's steps creaking on the floor behind her.

"The lectern," Ezekiel said. "Bring me to the lectern."

"So you've been here before."

Eliza's comment went unanswered. Big Jack did as he was told and placed him on top of the lectern, in lieu of a book. Eliza shuddered at the sight. She still couldn't get used to the sight of a disembodied head that made expressions and talked. It looked like a special effect, as if he must be hiding inside the lectern with his head coming out the top. Of all the supernatural things she had witnessed, this one was the most uncanny. Thus far.

"Look inside," Ezekiel ordered Big Jack, who grunted, rooted around inside the lectern, and pulled out an ancient book bound in strange leather. Something about the book set off warning bells in Eliza's mind.

"What are you up to?"

"I said I wasn't going to employ necromancy," Ezekiel said. "But I'm afraid I won't be much use helping Jack as nothing but a head. Come along, Big Jack. Take me to the graveyard. And bring a shovel."

Big Jack opened up a closet to the side of altar and picked up a shovel.

"Just a minute," Eliza said, before he closed the door. Something had caught her eye. She walked into the closet and came out again wearing a hooded cloak that came down almost to her ankles. It was scarlet.

"Pretty," Big Jack said.

"Well, well," Ezekiel said.

Eliza bowed. Then she picked up the guitar case and started for the door. "Come on then. We've got black magic to do."

Behind the church was a graveyard that was older than Methusalah.

Many of the names were familiar: Cock Robin, Old Mother Hubbard, Ephraim Pratt . . . Then they came to a simple slate gravestone carved in traditional New England fashion with a skull with angel wings. It seemed an abomination to desecrate such beauty. But desecrate it they did. Big Jack planted his shovel in the cold earth and dug by the light of the full moon. Graverobbing was slow work, and to pass the time Eliza pulled the black guitar from its case and began to strum the strings idly. The strings shone silver in the moonlight, and a sudden inspiration stuck her.

> Cold blows the wind, tonight, true love;
>   Cold fall the drops the rain;
> I only had but one true love;
>   In Greenwood she lies slain.
>
> 'I'll do as much for my true love,
>   As any young man may;
> I'll sit and mourn upon her grave
>   For twelvemonth and a day.'
>
> And when a year and day had gone,
>   The ghost began to weep.
> 'Why do you sit upon my grave
>   And do not let me sleep?'
>
> 'There is one thing I want, my love,
>   Just one thing that I crave;
> I crave one kiss from your cold lips,
>   Then I'll go from your grave.'
>
> 'But lily, lily are my lips;
>   My breath is earthy strong.

> If you would kiss my clay-cold lips,
>   Your days would not be long.
>
> 'Go down to yonder garden green,
>   Love, where we used to walk;
> The fairest rose that e'er was seen
>   Has withered to the stalk.
>
> 'The stalk is withered dry, true love,
>   As do our hearts decay;
> So rest yourself in peace, true love,
>   Till Death calls you away.'

The deed was done and a coffin unearthed. Inside the coffin, which was shaped like a long hexagon, was a headless skeleton clothed in tattered antique finery—the black frock coat and white tie of a clergyman. Big Jack propped Ezekiel's head upon a crypt and opened the book for him to read the terrible words.

There was terrible creaking sound. The bones in the coffin reassembled themselves and rose from the grave by the power of necromantic puppetry. Eliza watched, doubting her sanity as the horrible thing strode across the graveyard in the shimmering moonlight and picked up its head, which it reattached to its body. Ezekiel Whitlock was whole once more, though at a ghastly cost. With his skeletal fingers, he buttoned his collar and adjusted his tie in an attempt to hide the monstrosity beneath his clothes.

"Desperate times call for desperate measures," he said.

"I'm not judging you," Eliza replied.

"Lovely song, by the way. I didn't know you knew how to play."

"Neither did I. So what now?"

"Now we must go looking for Jack."

"I thought he went into that house we saw."

"Alas, we cannot follow him there. That path is for him alone. We'll need to take the long way around."

"Which is?"

"You'll see. Childe Eliza to the dark tower came . . . perhaps. Doesn't quite scan, does it? Never mind."

Big Jack returned the crimson book to the church, which he locked carefully, and then led Eliza and the now-mobile Ezekiel through the wood until they arrived at the shore of vast lake. The surface of the lake was swirling with mist, and much as she tried to peer through it, Eliza could not see the other side.

A black ship emerged from the mist. It was as black as black could be, with tattered black sails. Upon its deck stood an eldritch mariner. And then Ezekiel and Eliza were on the deck with him. Big Jack remained on the shore. He was the keeper of the church and couldn't leave Hexham. The mariner and the clergyman regarded each other for long moment and then clasped each other in the embrace of old friends. Then the mariner turned his gaze towards Eliza.

"Cotsplut!" he said. "If it isn't the spit and image of Jack. But Jack as a girl."

"Captain, allow me to introduce–" Ezekiel began.

"Scarlett," she finished. "Scarlett Cloake."

– XXIX –
BLACK STAR

The clocks were striking all thirteen—
    The Goblin-Prince had gone,
While all around a silver sheen
    Of dancing moonlight shone,

And on the shore our heroes stood
    Beside a velvet sea,
Whose depths held dreams both bad and good,
    Which never came to be.

Upon those inky waters rode
    A ship with tattered sails,
Whose supernatural presence bode
    The darkest of travails.

The ship was known by many names—
    The Raven, and Black Star . . .
Her captain liked to play cruel games,
    For he had sailed too far.

They climbed aboard with open eyes
    As wide as they could be,
And saw a black star shine above,
    Which blackly lit the sea.

How can this be, you well may ask—
    How can a black star light?
It was a light we cannot see,
    But penetrates the night.

Well, there were many vortices
    That drag men far below,
To unmourned graves beneath the waves
    Beyond the endless flow.

The laws of space were stretched too thin
    Upon this violent sea;
The Black Star's sails with phantom winds
    Expanded from the lee.

The Black Star passed into the mist,
    Which bounded all of Dreame,
And so they passed beyond the veil,
    The rational extreme.

All logic here turned inside out,
    Here in the Land of Nod,
A gloomy insubstantial realm,
    Where ruled a Hidden God.

They lit upon a black-lit shore
    Upon a spectral isle,
A place which reason must abhor
    And sanity revile.

Their journey done, they disembarked,
  Yᵉ Black Star sailed away—
Abandoned in the Land of Nod,
  Where Nightmare's ravens play.

XXIX. Black Star

– XXX –
The Dream-Quest of Unknown Jack

Yᵉ Labyrinth holds many twists,
    And at its heart a flow'r–
The very heart of what exists,
    A dark and ancient tow'r.

A titan race this scheme designed
    To guard an ark-held stone,
Which fell to earth when stars aligned
    And made the heavens groan.

Three walkers strode Yᵉ Labyrinth,
    A red, a white, a black,
Who wandered each one deeper in
    In search of unknown Jack.

The red one's name was Scarlett Cloake,
    A most resourceful girl,
Whose tale was told by many folk,
    Her skin as wan as pearl.

Old Whitelocke was a wizard who
    Once preached of Mother Goose,
Until he fell from favour due
    To sorcerous abuse.

The last one wore a shepherd's hood
    As black as darkest night;
His many names were understood—
    To speak one would be trite.

Each took a path with many turns,
    But never once they crossed;
And each who walked was searching for
    A love that had been lost.

Young Scarlett was the first to reach
    Y^e Tower's oaken gate;
Its passages had much to teach
    About the twists of fate.

She opened up the oaken door,
    A-turning Silver Key,
To peel a layer near the core,
    Which still she could not see.

Here halls of polished crimson wood
    Still drew her deeper in
This maze of lies devoid of good,
    This labyrinth of sin.

Until she reached its cold dead heart
    And found the other two;
The white and black ones stood apart,
    While o'er a raven flew.

It was a tiny garret room,
    Y^e Tower's very top,
Which held the stillness of a tomb;
    All time there seemed to stop.

A skeleton slumped at a desk,
    A quill pen in his hand—
A fiendish horror so grotesque,
    She lost her mind's command.

A crimson book the dead man wrote;
    Y^e Shepherd took it up,
And brushing off its dusty coat,
    He drank then from Y^e Cup.

The moonlight cast a spectral sheen
    Upon this puppet stage;
What audience this play had seen
    Perplexed the wisest mage.

Y^e Shepherd's hood was lowered down,
    Revealing grinning Jack—
A tattered overall-clad clown
    Beneath the robes of black.

Then he and Scarlett shared a kiss,
    While Whitelocke dealt them done;
And one day they would reminisce
    Of times past with their son.

The Eldritch Mariner

– XXXI –
The Rime of the Eldritch Mariner

The greatest mercy in the world,
    I think, is we are blind
To contents that lie tightly furled,
    Asleep within the mind.

Well, it was at a wedding feast
    Where I was next of kin;
A host of fishy relatives
    The church had just gone in,

When did a staring lunatic
    Upon me lay a hand;
His beard grew like a prickly thorn,
    His face in tropics tanned.

It was an Eldritch Mariner,
    Made hoary in short years,
For he had seen with his own eyes
    What lurks in darkest fears.

That is not dead, he raved to me,
    Which can eternal lie;
And æons' strangeness may one day
    Cause even death to die.

It started with a raven that
    Had roosted on the mast.
I tried to disregard its caws,
    Which drove me mad at last.

We sailed in fœtid southern seas,
    In waters thick as ooze,
The constellations alien,
    Our consolation booze.

'Twas on a drunken sleepless night
    That I took up my gun
To shoot the raven through the heart,
    And so the deal was done.

Mayhap it was grim Odin's bird
    That recklessly I'd slain,
And it was then the ocean groaned
    As if it were in pain.

The latitude and longitude
    I'll carry to my tomb,
For it was there a city rose
    Where sleeps our race's doom.

My crewmates' faces turned pale white,
    Just like that maiden Death,
Who kisses you with blood-red lips
    And steals your final breath.

We lit upon the island's shore
    Of slime-slick stones and mud,
And staggered through a ruin that
    Gushed terrors in a flood.

Across the titan masonry
    We crawled like tiny ants;
And what we saw there made us know
    The solace nescience grants.

Vast horrors lay beneath those stones—
    Of that there was no doubt;
Their angles joined impossibly
    To Euclid's theorems flout.

We crossed the courtyard in a daze,
    A monstrous marketplace;
With revelations there we saw
    Our minds could not keep pace.

It was the Portugee who climbed
    That dæmoniac stair
To call us in a hoarsened voice
    With wild dishevelled hair.

A Cyclops's door to hellish depths
    Before us towered high;
To call our actions reasonable
    Would be to tell a lie.

Without result we pushed the door,
    Until the answer dawned:
It hinged on a diagonal—
    And like a maw it yawned.

The aperture was raven-black
    And spewed out horrid things,
Which long had been imprisoned there
    And flew on filmy wings.

The odour was unbearable;
    We heard a slopping sound,
As something lumbered towards the door,
    From far beneath the ground.

Cthulhu now was loose again
    And ravened for delight,
Asleep a vigintillion years.
    Abhorrent was the sight,

For now the stars were right again;
    A mountain stumbled blind—
A sticky star-spawned bat-winged god
    Before us did we find.

And what an age-old cult had failed
    By artifice to do
Accomplished then by accident
    A random foolish crew.

Its flabby claws swept up three men
    Before they even turned;
God rest their souls if there be rest,
    And not from heaven spurned.

We plunged in terror over rocks
    Whose angles most perplexed;
And in the end but two survived
    To witness what came next.

My mate and I fled in the ship
    As fast as she could steam;
The creature cursed us from the shore
    Just like the Polypheme.

The Thing was bold and would not stop;
    It slid into the sea.
The churning claimed my crewmate's mind,
    And soon a corpse was he.

A desperate gamble I took then,
    And so reversed my course
To speed towards the noxious Thing
    And strike with lethal force.

Relentlessly I drove the bow
    Through jelly foul and green,
Which burst and smelt of open graves,
    Abhorrently unclean.

I heard a seething sound astern—
    The sky-spawn recombined;
But then our distance widened fast
    Before I lost my mind.

So now I've told my loathsome tale
    In hopes my soul to shrive;
And yet I fear I will be cursed
    As long as I'm alive.

Water, water, everywhere,
    Cthulhu dreams below;
R'lyeh wgah'nagl fhtagn:
    This blasphemy I know.

The Wedding-Guest then turned away,
    Made mad from what he'd learned;
And like the Eldritch Mariner
    His soul now heaven spurned.

– XXXII –
An Ancient Tomb A-Yonder Lies

My name is Jack; you've heard of me,
    For I once climbed a bean
That sprouted like a cosmic tree
    Beyond the world that's seen.

The gold I robbed from giants' hoards,
    I'd squandered long ago;
And so I roamed the earth in search
    Of ways to score more dough.

One autumn night I rolled into
    A town called Dunwich, Mass.,
A dreary godforsaken place,
    Where I had stopped for gas.

I did not plan to stop there long—
    Just quickly fill my tank;
But when the steam rose from the hood,
    My heart that moment sank.

Forsaking then the heap I drove,
    I set off towards the town;
And hoped I'd find a tavern where
    My sorrows I could drown.

Abandon Hope the bar was called,
    A dismal little dive,
Where whisky soon conspired to
    My common sense deprive.

A stranger sidled up to me,
    His face hid by a beard;
I tried hard not to shrink from him—
    His musk was strong and weird.

'My name is Whateley,' he declared,
    His voice a Yankee whine;
'Your advent is a timely one,
    For constellations line.'

'Who, me?' I answered, sipping rye.
    'I'm just a country boy;
But go ahead and spin your yarn,
    For fables are my joy.'

'It is no fable,' Whateley roared,
    And pounded with his fist.
'For I have seen sepulchral things
    Which ought not to exist.'

He handed me a silver key
    That I had seen before;
It opened up a door to dreams,
    Which reason must abhor.

'An ancient tomb a-yonder lies,
    A mile's walk down the road;
Go open it and you will learn
    The doom that heavens bode.'

So I struck out to find this tomb,
    Although I knew not why;
Perhaps it was the silver moon
    Ascendant in the sky.

And on the road I met a man
    Who had a single eye;
A grey beard dangled from his chin,
    And yet his step was spry.

'Say, cousin, could you spare a dime?'
    The old man cleared his throat;
I reached into my overalls,
    And found a silver groat.

I placed it in the greybeard's palm
    Without a second thought;
The last one of the giant's hoard,
    For which I'd bravely fought.

I tipped my battered rainwet hat
    And turned to go my way;
The old man grabbed my flannel's sleeve
    And stopped me then to say,

'Your kindness is your saving grace,
    For I am Nodens named;
Now take this charm and it will save
    Your soul from being claimed.'

He pressed an amulet into
    My giant-killer's grip,
An elder sign in silver wrought,
    Which would me well equip.

A graveyard stood outside of town,
    A long abandoned place;
And in the thorn I found the tomb
    In moss's soft embace.

Long centuries the tomb had lain
    And wisely left to rot;
Until I trespassed recklessly,
    For cautious I was not.

I turned the silver key inside
    The rusted eldritch lock,
For I was always of the mind
    To deal with things post hoc.

Quite empty was the tomb inside,
    Though foetid was its smell;
And then a panel opened which
    Revealed stairs down to Hell.

I took the stairs by twos and threes,
    And by their foot a lamp;
I lit it with my final match—
    A feat, for it was damp.

A passageway then lured me on
    Until I reached a room;
Inside a pile of mouldered bones,
    The bowels of the tomb.

And in a skeleton's last grasp,
    A ruby cold and red;
I prized it from his bony claw,
    Which held fast though long dead.

And knowing not to linger there,
    I dashed back towards the stair;
But blocking now my egress was
    A corpse with golden hair.

'That ruby is my beating heart,'
    The ghastly maiden screamed;
The sight was unbelievable—
    I wondered if I dreamed.

A desperate ploy I then devised,
    And took her in my arms;
For even Death's own bride could not
    Resist my rakish charms.

We twirled and swayed, a danse macabre,
    To piping strange and shrill;
I pulled her close and kissed her long,
    Which gave my loins a thrill.

Into the maiden's breast I pressed
    The hexfoil I had won;
She fell into a bony heap,
    Her night of dancing done.

By foot from Dunwich I made haste,
    As rosy fingers streamed;
The ruby in my pocket beat
    Just like a heart it seemed.

– XXXIII –
Yᴇ Jack of War

'Tis said when Hexham is in need
    To beat upon a drum,
When mountains groan and heavens bleed,
    For that's when Jack will come.

In yonder mountain stooped and old,
    There sleeps a Hidden God,
Whose stories are in whispers told,
    For he is King of Nod.

His messenger is dark of skin
    And has a braided beard;
Most disconcerting is his grin,
    Which bodes of something weird.

One night he walked into an inn
    Where way forked out from way,
Where many came to drink and sin,
    And balladeers to play.

His presence filled the inn with gloom;
    A veil of silence fell,
As utter as within a tomb
    Beneath Yᵉ Stranger's spell.

A red-cloaked minstrel played her song
    Upon a black guitar;
It was not very overlong,
    And was a tad bizarre.

The Devil came to Hexham Town
    And had a cruel design,
For he had journeyed from far down
    And craved a glass of wine.

But no amount of wine could quell
    His sorrow, black as ink;
Just what it was he could not tell,
    And so he took a drink.

Now Jack into the tavern strode,
    The grinning Ettinfell;
His boots were muddy from the road,
    Which led straight up from Hell.

He made his way up to the bar,
    A-thirsting for an ale;
He too had travelled very far
    And longed for a wassail.

There he and Nyarlathotep
    Were fated to cross ways;
Jack measured words not to misstep
    In how he formed his phrase.

'I am the mighty Ettinfell,
      Extolled in tale and song,
For I have braved the depths of Hell
      Where suffering is long.'

'You gnat, you worm, you earthly man!'
      Y^e Stranger gave a laugh.
'Your life is such a trifling span,
      An instant cut in half.'

'King Marock waits for you at home
      At crumbling Ettinfell;
For it was written in Y^e Tome
      That he would come to dwell.'

So spake Y^e Stranger with the beard,
      Who raised Jack's hackles high;
He knew the final battle neared,
      And that a king must die.

Jack hied himself into Y^e Wood
      (Though first he quaffed his ale);
He knew that it was understood
      That he must never fail.

He made his way into the thorn
      Which hid an old white church,
For it was here that he was born,
      And easy was his search.

The church's door then opened for
    Jack's eldritch silver key,
The musty smell evoking yore,
    When but a boy was he.

The windows held glass images,
    Depicting wars of old,
Of angels fighting scrimmages
    With those who'd left the fold.

One dæmon bore the blackest wings,
    Which spread across the sky,
An omen of the doom he brings
    To those who cheat and lie.

King Lucifer this devil's name,
    His hair of flowing gold,
His face and Jack's were much the same,
    Or so the tale was told.

This picture held Jack's searching gaze;
    He knew it was his weird
To wander deep into the maze
    Where Lucifer appeared.

But like the hero in the myth,
    Jack aimed to kill the beast,
And so resolved to go forthwith
    Before his will decreased.

He opened up a closet door,
    Wherein a sword was leant
Against a wall long years before,
    Until a knight was sent.

But this was not just any sword,
    Its blade unearthly keen;
By giant-kind it was abhorred—
    To them, it was obscene.

Jack took it up and strapped it on,
    The sword snug in its sheath;
He drew it then to swear upon,
    While dæmons quaked beneath.

'I call myself Yᵉ Jack of War
    And fight in Arthur's name,
Dishonoured by a wanton whore,
    Who brought my kindred shame.

'I vow to knock upon the door
    Which guards the crumbling manse
My ancestor built years before,
    Where shades of dead Drakes dance.

'And if this man, this low-born king,
    Will not give up his claim,
Then I his fate to him will bring,
    Or Jack is not my name.'

So with his pledge, this flaming Jack
    Struck out into Y^e Wood,
While watching him enrobed in black,
    Y^e Stranger, under hood.

Sir Jack arrived at Ettinfell,
    Which was not very far,
And distant tolled a sombre knell
    While flashing by, a star.

To his surprise, his wife was there
    To greet him at the door,
Pure gold her flowing dress and hair,
    The Pixy-Queen of lore.

'I aim to strike King Marock dead,'
    Jack told her, grim his tone.
'With this sharp blade I'll lop his head—
    Do not my quest postpone.'

'But I have laid a feast so grand
    For Father and for you;
Why, surely you can stay your hand
    A while and still be true.'

Well, Jack he let himself be swayed
    By fragrant hair grown wild,
His noble quest for now allayed
    By how a woman smiled.

The dining hall of Ettinfell
    Was great as it was wide;
Here Arthur once had feasted well
    A host of knights inside.

But now there was just Marock here,
    With Leah and Sir Jack;
While at the window strained to hear
    Y^e Stranger robed in black.

'I fear you aim to take my head,'
    Said Marock with a laugh.
'Why don't you slice some meat instead?
    Pour wine from this carafe.'

Jack feasted well and went to bed;
    His quest could wait till morn.
He'd use his sword for love instead,
    And prick a rose with thorn.

And when he woke the house was gone,
    A crumbling pile of stone;
Jack lay in moss in breaking dawn,
    Dew-covered and alone.

And so he hied upon a whim
    To misty old Lake Nod;
A ship arrived to carry him
    To meet the Hidden God.

```
      *
      *
    * * *
      *
```

A.D.
2017

Acknowledgments

"The Ballad of Jack Keeper," *Spectral Realms* No. 2 (Winter 2015), Hippocampus Press.

"The Black Cup," "The Lay of Jackson Drake," "The Dream Emerald," "The Broken Promise," "Gooseberry Tea," "Jack the Hunter," and "Fiddler Jack," *The Fall of the House of Drake* (2015), Dunhams Manor Press.

"The Lay of Jackson Drake" (as "Childe Jackson Drake"), *Spectral Realms* No. 3 (Summer 2015), Hippocampus Press.

"The Hidden God" (extract from "The Dream Emerald"), *Spectral Realms* No. 1 (Summer 2014), Hippocampus Press.

"Fiddler Jack," *Spectral Realms* No. 4 (Winter 2016), Hippocampus Press.

"Y^e Yellow'd Reed," *Xnoybis #3: In Praise of Pan* (2017), Dunhams Manor Press.

"The Devil's Lanthorn," *Halloween Howlings*, Rainfall Books (2015).

"The Rime of the Eldritch Mariner," *Spectral Realms* No. 5 (Summer 2016), Hippocampus Press; *The 2017 Rhysling Anthology* (2017), Science Fiction Poetry Association (Rhysling Award winner, Long Poem, Second Place).